intervoice

TWENTY YEARS OF INNOVATION

intervoice
TWENTY YEARS OF INNOVATION

RICHARD F. HUBBARD & **JEFFREY L. RODENGEN**

Edited by Jon VanZile
Design and layout by Dennis Shockley & Rachelle Donley

With love to Robyn, Maren, and Lauren—you are my life.

—Richard F. Hubbard

WRITE STUFF

Write Stuff Enterprises, Inc.
1001 South Andrews Avenue
Second Floor
Fort Lauderdale, FL 33316
1-800-900-Book (1-800-900-2665)
(954) 462-6657
www.writestuffbooks.com

Publisher's Cataloging in Publication

Hubbard, Richard F.
    Intervoice: twenty years of innovation/
Richard F. Hubbard & Jeffrey L. Rodengen;
edited by Jon VanZile; design and layout by
Dennis Shockley & Rachelle Donley. — 1st ed.
    p. cm.
    Includes bibliographical references and index.

LCCN 2001135152
ISBN 0-945903-88-X

    1. Intervoice (firm) — History. 2. Speech
processing systems industry — United States —
History. 3. Telecommunication equipment
industry — United States — History.
I. Rodengen, Jeffrey L. II. Title

HD9696.S44I58 2003   338.4'7621399
                            QBI03-200366

Also by Jeffrey L. Rodengen

The Legend of Chris-Craft

IRON FIST: The Lives of Carl Kiekhaefer

Evinrude-Johnson and The Legend of OMC

Serving the Silent Service: The Legend of Electric Boat

The Legend of Dr Pepper/Seven-Up

The Legend of Honeywell

The Legend of Briggs & Stratton

The Legend of Ingersoll-Rand

The Legend of Stanley: 150 Years of The Stanley Works

The MicroAge Way

The Legend of Halliburton

The Legend of York International

The Legend of Nucor Corporation

The Legend of Goodyear: The First 100 Years

The Legend of AMP

The Legend of Cessna

The Legend of VF Corporation

The Spirit of AMD

The Legend of Rowan

New Horizons: The Story of Ashland Inc.

The History of American Standard

The Legend of Mercury Marine

The Legend of Federal-Mogul

Against the Odds: Inter-Tel—The First 30 Years

The Legend of Pfizer

State of the Heart: The Practical Guide to Your Heart and Heart Surgery
with Larry W. Stephenson, M.D.

The Legend of Worthington Industries

The Legend of Trinity Industries, Inc.

The Legend of IBP, Inc.

The Legend of Cornelius Vanderbilt Whitney

The Legend of Amdahl

The Legend of Litton Industries

The Legend of Gulfstream

The Legend of Bertram
with David A. Patten

The Legend of Ritchie Bros. Auctioneers

The Legend of ALLTEL
with David A. Patten

The Yes, you can of Invacare Corporation
with Anthony L. Wall

The Ship in the Balloon: The Story of Boston Scientific and the Development of Less-Invasive Medicine

The Legend of Day & Zimmermann

The Legend of Noble Drilling

Fifty Years of Innovation: Kulicke & Soffa

Biomet—From Warsaw to the World
with Richard F. Hubbard

NRA: An American Legend

The Heritage and Values of RPM, Inc.

The Marmon Group: The First Fifty Years

The Legend of Grainger

The Legend of The Titan Corporation
with Richard F. Hubbard

The Legend of Discount Tire
with Richard F. Hubbard

The Legend of La-Z-Boy
with Richard F. Hubbard

The Legend of McCarthy
with Richard F. Hubbard

Completely produced in the
United States of America
10 9 8 7 6 5 4 3 2 1

TABLE OF CONTENTS

Foreword by Alan Bean vi

Acknowledgments viii

PART I

Chapter I   The Seeds of Innovation 12

Chapter II   The Early Years 28

Chapter III   InterVoice Grows Up 40

Chapter IV   An Open Vision 60

PART II

Chapter V   Brite Voice: The Early Years 78

Chapter VI   Gaining Ground 90

PART III

Chapter VII   The InterVoice-Brite Merger 106

Chapter VIII   Technology Talks 116

Chapter IX   Two Decades and Beyond 130

Notes to Sources 138

Index 148

FOREWORD

by
Alan Bean
Former Apollo astronaut

AMERICA'S CONQUEST OF the moon is studded with tense moments and milestones, setbacks, and small victories. It remains perhaps humanity's most enduring technological accomplishment, an exercise in teamwork that took a nation to accomplish.

As the fourth man on the moon and later commander of the Skylab, I had the opportunity to observe firsthand how a dedicated group of professionals can accomplish almost anything, even walking on the moon. It was a lesson in leadership, teamwork, imagination, intellect, and sheer perseverance that I will never forget. Or perhaps put a better way, it was thousands of smaller lessons.

One of these object lessons occurred during the Apollo 16 mission, several years after the celebrated moon landing of Neil Armstrong. While orbiting the moon in their lunar module, preparing for descent, astronauts John Young and Charlie Duke received an unsettling call from Ken Mattingly, in the command module. Mattingly reported an unexpected oscillation in the backup steering system for the rocket engine. It was a serious situation. If the oscillation prevented the backup system from properly steering the rocket, all three astronauts would have to return to earth as soon as possible. Worse yet, if the primary and backup systems failed, the men would have been stuck orbiting the moon forever.

Immediately, more than 200,000 miles away, engineers at mission control in Houston and from California to Florida began to work the problem, building simulations and running the numbers, all the time asking themselves the crucial question: Would the oscillations prevent the backup system from working? Finally, less than six hours later, they arrived at an answer: The oscillations would damp out as rocket thrust built up at engine start. The word was given, and the mission continued successfully.

Years later, I painted a picture of that proud, but not very well known, moment in American space travel. I painted astronaut John Young as he stood on the moon, proudly saluting the American flag. I called this picture *An American Success Story*.

I chose this powerful title because Young's salute had greater meaning than one man in front of one flag. Rather, his salute captured the spirit of the astronauts who flew with him, the thousands of engineers and support personnel who made their flight possible, and the millions of Americans who supported our space program. He saluted teamwork, creativity, and hard work.

These qualities have not lost their luster in the ensuing decades. America is a country built on cooperation and enthusiasm and on leadership. Whether we're talking about the space program, our governmental systems, or corporations like Intervoice, excellence demands creative and qualified people who are given the time and resources to do their jobs. Success further requires that each of these individuals work toward a common goal, united behind leadership that keeps a vigilant eye on long-term strategy.

In 1997, I was present when Intervoice launched its own Apollo project. Known as InterSoft, it was software that allowed programmers to write voice applications for any computer operating system. It was an important technological moment for the company, but that's not really why I was there. Rather, I was there to talk about leadership and vision, two qualities I saw at Intervoice. This is a company that looked into the technological marketplace and saw an opportunity to create innovative voice application products. Then it set about patiently designing and moving these new applications into industries that had never seen them before, including banking and government agencies.

This kind of perseverance distinguishes all great American success stories. In the space program, there were literally thousands of errors, and the road to the moon was a different

An American Success Story

road than we expected. Yet no one could argue with our results, and therein lies the key to success. We planned on success but expected challenges that would require us to be flexible. In the end, nothing was allowed to deter us from the moon.

It is, of course, difficult to withstand this kind of pressure, and that's where leadership comes in. At NASA, we were fortunate to have superior, seasoned

leadership. There were times when the younger people in the program, including myself, would become discouraged. Our task was immensely complicated and required that tens of thousands of elements work in perfect harmony. Yet perfect harmony is impossible; people aren't perfect, and neither are the machines we create. Still our leaders never wavered. They would simply try to understand what really happened and how to prevent it from happening again. Every step of our moon mission involved constant refinement—even up to the point of landing on the moon.

During the Apollo 11 moon landing, the alarms went off. These alarms had never sounded before, even during hundreds of simulations. It was an unforeseen challenge. Yet it turned out the problem was only something to do with the rendezvous radar. At the time, no one knew why the alarm would trigger right then as opposed to any other time, but what mattered was that it didn't affect the landing. It was only a glitch, one of those things that happens. Leadership recognizes that glitches will happen and plans for them by moving resources around within an organization or pushing teams down parallel paths to see which is best. Good leadership is focused on results; one way or another, we were going to the moon.

These are the very same qualities that I see at Intervoice. Like all successful organizations, Intervoice is not afraid to blaze trails, to work problems one step at a time, and to exercise the kind of leadership that is necessary to bring even the most impossible goals to fruition.

ACKNOWLEDGMENTS

A GREAT NUMBER OF PEOPLE ASSISTED in the research, preparation, and publication of *Intervoice: Twenty Years of Innovation.*

This book would not have been possible without the devoted skills of our research assistant Lindsey Townsend. Her exhaustive survey of the company's archives was indispensible to the book's success. Jon VanZile, executive editor, oversaw the text and photos from beginning to end, and Dennis Shockley, art director, brought the story to life with his eye for design.

At Intervoice, special thanks are due to David Brandenburg, chief executive officer, and Dan Hammond, former chief executive officer. These two devoted a great deal of valuable time to revising and checking the text for accuracy. The authors are deeply indebted to them for sharing the spirit of the Intervoice story. Similarly, Intervoice President Bob Ritchey provided key insight to the company's strategy and future.

Several other people provided crucial assistance to the book during its development. Particular among these was Stephanie Leonard, manager, Global Public relations, who was extremely helpful in the final stages, organizing both text and artwork. Jim Gardner, director of Marketing, also lent his expertise to the project.

Many other Intervoice executives, employees, retirees, friends, and family members greatly enriched the book by dicussing their experiences and lending valued photos from their personal collections.

The authors extend their particular gratitude to Mike Barker, Bogdan Blaszczak, Stan Brannan, Don Brown, Skip Cave, Don Crosbie, Glenn Etherington, Craig Evans, Don Evans, Al Fleener, Pete Foster, Marc Gardner, Gordon Givens, Rob-Roy Graham, Keith Gyssler, Kathy Hackney, Myra Hambleton, Dwain Hammond, Dean Howell, Walt Mirkowicz, Ray Naeini, Tuan Nguyen, Joe Pietropaolo, George Platt Sr., Mike Polcyn, Cynthia Rivers, Abhay Sawant, David Tannenbaum, Chris Tessarowicz, Mike Tessarowicz, Phil Walden, and Scotty Walsh.

As always, special thanks are extended to the dedicated staff at Write Stuff Enterprises, Inc.: Melody Maysonet, senior editor; Heather Deeley, associate editor; Bonnie Freeman, copyeditor; Sandy Cruz, senior art director; Rachelle Donley and Wendy Iverson, art directors; Mary Aaron, transcriptionist; Barb Koch, indexer; Bruce Borich, production manager; Marianne Roberts, vice president of administration; Sherry Hasso, bookkeeper; Linda Edell, executive assistant to Jeffrey L. Rodengen; Lars Jessen, director of worldwide marketing; Irena Xanthos, manager of sales, promotions, and advertising; Rory Schmer, distribution supervisor; and Jennifer Walter, administrative assistant.

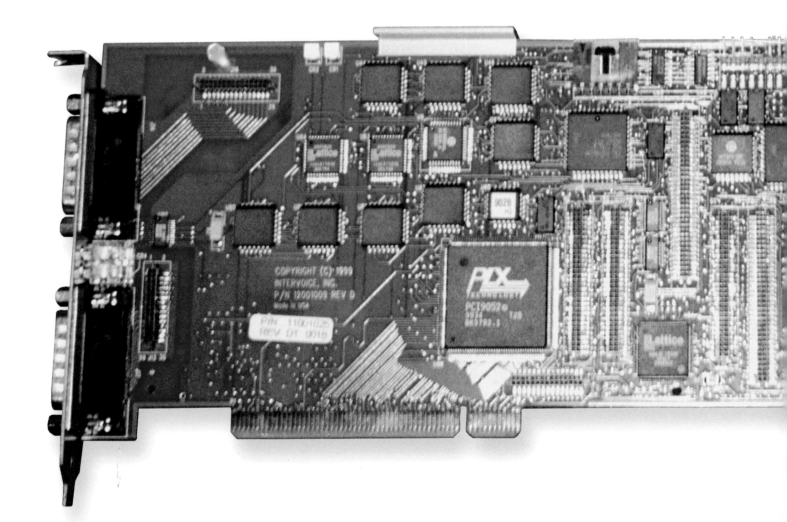

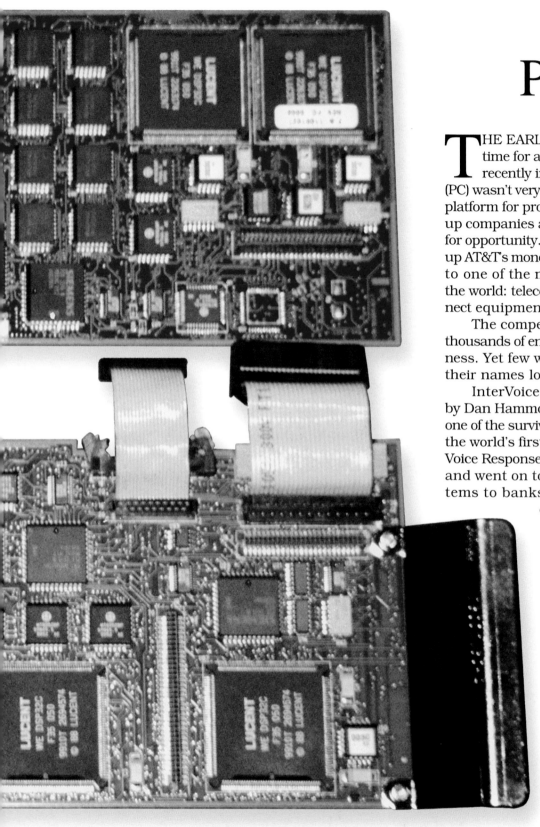

PART I

THE EARLY 1980S WAS AN EXCITING time for any engineer. Even though the recently introduced personal computer (PC) wasn't very sophisticated, it offered a new platform for product development, and start-up companies across America began to look for opportunity. Then in 1984, the FCC broke up AT&T's monopoly, throwing open the doors to one of the most lucrative industries in the world: telecommunications and interconnect equipment.

The competitive crush was enormous; thousands of entrepreneurs rushed into business. Yet few would stand the test of time, their names lost to history.

InterVoice, founded in Dallas in 1983 by Dan Hammond and Mike Tessarowicz, is one of the survivors. The company introduced the world's first PC-based digital Interactive Voice Response (IVR) system for a telephone and went on to sell thousands of IVR systems to banks, retail outlets, insurance companies, government agencies, and many other institutions. Along the way, InterVoice grew quickly, overcoming the issues common to growing companies and becoming a technology leader in its industry.

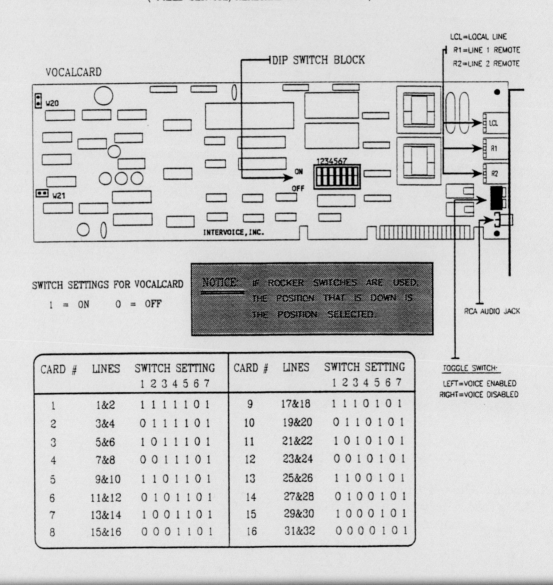

InterVoice VOCALCARD®
Setup Guide
For DIP Switches

INTERVOICE, INC.
1850 N. GREENVILLE AVE. STE 184
RICHARDSON, TEXAS, 75081

IBM
Authorized
Value Added
Dealer

*** PLEASE RETAIN FOR FUTURE REFERENCE ***

(FIELD SERVICE/REALCARE 800-346-6244)

LCL=LOCAL LINE
R1=LINE 1 REMOTE
R2=LINE 2 REMOTE

DIP SWITCH BLOCK

VOCALCARD

W20

1234567
ON
OFF

LCL

R1

R2

W21

INTERVOICE, INC.

RCA AUDIO JACK

SWITCH SETTINGS FOR VOCALCARD

1 = ON   0 = OFF

NOTICE: IF ROCKER SWITCHES ARE USED, THE POSITION THAT IS DOWN IS THE POSITION SELECTED.

TOGGLE SWITCH:
LEFT=VOICE ENABLED
RIGHT=VOICE DISABLED

CARD #	LINES	SWITCH SETTING 1 2 3 4 5 6 7	CARD #	LINES	SWITCH SETTING 1 2 3 4 5 6 7
1	1&2	1 1 1 1 1 0 1	9	17&18	1 1 1 0 1 0 1
2	3&4	0 1 1 1 1 0 1	10	19&20	0 1 1 0 1 0 1
3	5&6	1 0 1 1 1 0 1	11	21&22	1 0 1 0 1 0 1
4	7&8	0 0 1 1 1 0 1	12	23&24	0 0 1 0 1 0 1
5	9&10	1 1 0 1 1 0 1	13	25&26	1 1 0 0 1 0 1
6	11&12	0 1 0 1 1 0 1	14	27&28	0 1 0 0 1 0 1
7	13&14	1 0 0 1 1 0 1	15	29&30	1 0 0 0 1 0 1
8	15&16	0 0 0 1 1 0 1	16	31&32	0 0 0 0 1 0 1

A schematic for InterVoice's original VocalCard Setup Guide. The company was founded in 1983.

CHAPTER ONE

THE SEEDS OF INNOVATION

The Beginning–1985

Beware of programmers with screwdrivers.

— Anonymous

THE COMPANY THAT would eventually become InterVoice was, like so many successful technology companies, the fortunate outcome of vision, risk, and hard work.

Looking back, company cofounder Dan Hammond would credit three forces for InterVoice's success. The first was the 1968 Carterfone decision, which threw the telephone interconnect industry open to competition. The second was Touch-Tone technology, a 1960s AT&T innovation that allowed phones and telecommunications networks to communicate with computerized tones instead of human operators. The final element, and perhaps most important, was Interactive Voice Response (IVR), which allowed a combination of inputs, including human voice and Touch-Tone signals, to interact with a computerized phone system.

Like Touch-Tone, IVR was not a new phenomenon. IBM had pioneered the technology in the 1960s on a mainframe. It took another major development to put this tool within reach of hungry entrepreneurs: the personal computer (PC). In August 1981, IBM introduced its first IBM PC. Powered by DOS (Disk Operating System) and an Intel 8080 microprocessor, its price tag was $1,565. This IBM machine, built around a tiny microprocessor, was truly revolutionary. Gordon Moore, a cofounder of Intel, later described the first microprocessor as "one of the most revolutionary products in the history of mankind."[1]

The IBM personal computer offered extraordinary possibilities. Considering its size and the technological progress of the era, it had tremendous speed and computing capabilities for relatively little investment. And it was built from off-the-shelf parts: enterprising engineers could open up the box and adapt it to their own use.[2] In January 1983, *Time* magazine named the personal computer its "Man of the Year"—meaning *Time's* editors considered the computer the most influential newsmaker of 1982. Never before (or since) was an inanimate object chosen Man of the Year.

An Enterprising Pair

The same year the PC earned *Time's* nod as Man of the Year, Dan Hammond, vice president of a technology company called SD Systems, which built microcomputers, quit his job to pursue opportunities with the IBM PC.

While at SD Systems, Hammond met a software engineer named Mike Tessarowicz, who had come to the company when it was restructured as Syntech. Tessarowicz joined the company to write lottery

---

On February 26, 1985, the company changed its name to InterVoice Inc. shortly before its public offering. InterVoice was easier to remember than Interactive Technology Associates.

software. At Syntech, Tessarowicz worked on creating a lottery processing system for the Michigan Lottery; Hammond worked with him on the hardware side.

"We liked each other's work," Tessarowicz later said. "We worked together on some things, building a distributed processor where we wanted to process a very large lottery base using lots of microprocessors."[3]

Hammond also developed a line of desktop computers for SD Systems. He liked the technology of his desktop computers, but when the PC came out, he remembered looking at IBM's machine, then at his desktop computers (which, incidentally, were housed in blue boxes), and saying, "Hey, my blue computers aren't going to go anywhere now. I need to do something with a PC."[4]

The decision to quit his job and form a business based on the PC, however, was not an easy one. Since his graduation in 1973 from the University of Central Florida with a degree in electrical engineering, Hammond had worked for three computer companies, including SD Systems. An engineer at heart, he was not an obvious entrepreneur. The son of an aeronautical engineer who worked for Martin Marietta, Hammond had three children and had never run his own business. Nevertheless, he quit SD Systems "on a hope and a prayer" and formed Hammond Computer Products, a firm that developed computer products for the PC.

Tessarowicz quit shortly after and started a company called Transaction Technologies with financial backing from GTECH, a Rhode Island

Left: Dan Hammond, left, and Phil Walden, right, at SD Systems in 1979. Hammond was a vice president at SD Systems before he quit to run his own consulting business. Walden later became a vice president at InterVoice.

Right: Hammond, standing, gives a presentation in 1980 in Geneva, Switzerland, as an employee of SD Systems. While at the company, he designed microcomputer hardware and software.

gaming company for which Tessarowicz had worked before he moved to Texas. He and Hammond shared fourteen hundred square feet of office space at 1701 North Greenville Avenue in Richardson, Texas, and worked on early projects together.

"I accidentally stumbled onto a guy who said he needed a voice annotation system for a word processor," Tessarowicz said. "So Dan and I decided to put it together. Dan put together a board, and I put together software. But the big Southland order materialized. The result of it was that we had a little bit of a technology and we were familiar with the hardware and the software side of building speaking computers."[5]

Although they couldn't have known it, the two engineers picked a fortunate time to leave Syntech. Shortly after they left, the company, which was still making machines for the Michigan Lottery, was raided and shut down by Texas authorities. It turned out that Syntech was violating a century-old law in Texas that prohibited the manufacture of gambling equipment.

A Consulting Business

While he was looking for opportunities, Hammond faced the immediate concern of paying the bills and keeping food on his family's table. To earn some income, he launched a consulting practice on the side. It led him to Telephone Broadcast Systems (TBS), where an engineer named Skip Cave was vice president of engineering.

TBS, one of SD Systems' customers, used SD microcomputers to control automatic dialers coupled with voice recordings for marketing and bill collection. Customers were called and reminded by a taped voice recording that they had fallen behind in their payments. It was an early and crude form of IVR, operating on minicomputers, but it represented state-of-the-art technology at the time.

While at TBS, Cave had invented what may have been the world's first predictive dialer, a machine that dialed phone numbers from a list and could detect when a person answered the phone. If someone answered, the predictive dialer automatically routed the call to a telemarketing salesperson or played an automated message. In TBS's case, the system played prerecorded marketing or bill collection messages.

Shortly after leaving Syntech, Hammond landed a consulting contract with Cave to convert TBS's bank of audio tapes to a digital voice system. "Dan was looking for something to do, and I said, 'Why don't you come over and help us?'" Cave remembered.

He was a hardware engineer, and he had designed a lot of equipment for SD Systems. . . . My goal was to replace the cassette recorders that we had. We needed to get rid of those because they were unreliable. We wanted to automate the process and make it better and more efficient. So Dan and I talked, and I started a project to build the first digital enunciation system.[6]

Working together, Cave and Hammond created a digital version of the "junk phone call" machine—the TBS 1000. This product was successful for TBS, and in 1989, TBS was purchased by Davox, which wanted to enter the predictive dialing market. Davox developed into an industry leader.

A Voice Breakthrough

The TBS experience not only helped feed his family, it was valuable because it was the first time Hammond had worked on the "voice side" of his industry. Until then, he'd been working with interactive data systems, and he was intrigued by the possibilities of voice technology.

Throughout 1982 and into early 1983, Hammond and Tessarowicz talked about the possibility of building a voice system on the newly released IBM PC. It was a bold idea and not without a certain degree of risk. In hindsight, it's easy to see that the PC represented the vanguard of a boom in information and worker productivity that would define the 1990s economic miracle. But in 1983, all of this lay in the future, and many industry watchers considered the PC a sort of novel toy. It would be applicable for desktop applications, chorused the doubters, but as a high-powered tool for large corporations, the PC would always stand in the shadow of proven mainframes and minicomputers.

Nevertheless, Hammond and Tessarowicz remained convinced that the PC could be adapted for voice applications. They invested $50,000 of their own savings in a partnership to develop a revolutionary product: the world's first PC-based Interactive Voice Response system. It represented the natural evolution of all their previous efforts and talents. Tessarowicz wrote the software, and Hammond developed the boards. Cave consulted on the telephony side.

"This was a radical idea at the time," Cave remembered. "Nobody would ever have envisioned that you'd be able to do complicated things on a little PC."[7]

The Southland Deal

As Hammond remembered it, the first product they developed was a solution in search of a problem. "We didn't even really have a clue about what applications we were going to target," Hammond said.[8]

But it wouldn't take long for an opportunity to present itself. At the time, TBS sold systems to Southland, the parent corporation of the 7-Eleven convenience store chain. The Southland system used a predictive dialer to call people who had bounced checks at 7-Eleven. Once contact had been made, a message was delivered that the check had bounced and the customer had the opportunity to make good on the debt. While this system was effective, it wasn't optimized for incoming calls, meaning that store clerks couldn't call 7-Eleven's automated system for check authorization. What the convenience store wanted was a cost-effective check authorization system.

The Hammond family in the late 1960s. From left in the back row are Dan, Mac, Dwain, and Carol. Their parents, William and Volina, are in front. All three Hammond boys would work for InterVoice.

There were, of course, other check authorization services available. But they tended to rely on human operators who manually tracked down checking account balances. This sort of service didn't fit 7-Eleven's need. The convenience store had a lot of bad checks, but the typical 7-Eleven transaction wasn't very large. The average loss per check was only about a nickel, so it wasn't cost effective to use a service that cost more than that. Yet, because of the sheer volume of bad checks, 7-Eleven faced significant losses.

Both Hammond and Tessarowicz's systems addressed this need. Their system allowed store clerks to Touch-Tone in the customer's driver's license number and automatically receive a verbal check authorization number. All they needed was an entrée into the chain. It came in the form of

Martin Durbeck, a former vice president of sales for TBS. He saw their machine and said, "You know, it looks like you have something. I can probably sell it."[9] Before long, Durbeck had sold the system to 7-Eleven for check authorization.

In September 1983, Hammond and Tessarowicz founded a partnership called Interactive Technology Associates (ITA) to handle the Southland transaction. The company's first official employee was Tuan Nguyen, an engineer who had already been working for Tessarowicz at Transaction Technologies.

"I was really just out of college," Nguyen remembered. "Mike and I designed the software together. We had to write it in assembly language," he said, because of the computer's limitations at that time. "Everything had to fit into 64K of memory."[10]

The company's second employee was Ed Rivers, another engineer. "I interviewed for my job there in shorts," Rivers later recalled.

Within a week, I was working for Mike. It was a tiny office with a common hallway in the middle and four little rooms. One was Mike's office, one was Dan's office, one was a little lab, and then there was the lobby. Since they had no other place for me, I sat at the desk in the reception area.[11]

The first system, with the voice of Chris Tessarowicz, Mike's wife, on the prerecorded message, was installed in November 1983 in a Houston 7-Eleven. It paid for itself in less than a month by preventing acceptance of bad checks.

Although it had only one customer and was less than a year old, ITA felt the wind of optimism behind its sails. Southland itself was a huge opportunity, and selling to every store would represent a healthy little business. In fact, ITA would spend most of 1984 installing systems for 7-Eleven throughout the United States; it would eventually be used by four thousand of the stores.

But ITA's horizon was far broader than one chain of convenience stores. The company was positioned on the leading edge of a wave of interactive voice applications. Across the country, thousands of companies were paying tens of millions of dollars to human operators to handle routine requests that could be handled by a machine for

much less. Similarly, bill collectors and telemarketing companies would benefit from the technology. It was, to borrow a phrase from marketing textbooks, a "target rich" environment.

ITA was not the only company to recognize the massive potential of this unfolding market, of course. Other corporations and start-ups, such as Natural Microsystems, Rhetorics, and Dialogic, had the same goal of automating voice business. But ITA was unique in its business model because it was vertically integrated. The company built the boards, wrote the software, and installed the systems. The partners even developed their own programming language for their system. They called it InterVoice.

ITA Begins to Grow

From its earliest days, ITA was a company conceived and run by engineers. It had a spectacular product that was technically superior to its competitors'. But it didn't have much of a salesforce, and this was a weakness that Hammond and Tessarowicz recognized early on. In September 1984, while still installing systems for Southland, Hammond hired Don Crosbie as ITA's first director of sales and marketing.

Crosbie didn't exactly fit the mold of the typical sales executive; he had no sales experience. What he did have, however, was a personal touch. Crosbie had spent almost twenty years as a missionary in Asia, Indonesia, and the Philippines. He had traveled to more than seventy countries, directed mission organizations, and even run for Parliament in New Zealand.

When he was first offered the job, Crosbie demurred, saying he had no sales experience. But Hammond pressed him, saying, "You've been selling all your life—just a different product."[12] Finally, Crosbie relented and joined ITA as a regional manager with sales and marketing responsibilities. He would later serve as CFO.

Even as he transitioned into a sales and financial career, Crosbie never completely strayed from his past. As the company grew and added employees, Crosbie became something of an internal spiritual advisor. "It was always sort of known that my door was open if you have a personal problem," Crosbie remembered. Over the years, Crosbie even conducted weddings for a number of employees, including Dan Hammond and employees Mike Polcyn and Keith Gyssler.[13]

The challenge at ITA, however, was significantly less spiritual. Sales was a grueling, all-consuming task as ITA reached for new customers. Mailing campaigns, for example, were major projects, partially because laser printers could handle only two or three sheets a minute.

"I remember taking the printer home for the weekend, at the same time I was painting my house," Crosbie said.

I spent all weekend climbing up and down the ladder refilling the paper, running seven thousand letters. I also had to sign each one because we believed it was much more effective. So I'd sit there signing these seven thousand letters, and people would look at me as if I was crazy. But we were trying to do direct mail in a very personalized sense.[14]

As a former minister, Don Crosbie, the company's first director of sales and marketing, married several couples while at InterVoice, including Dan and Holly Hammond in August 1992. Gordon Givens, rear left, was Dan's best man.

The ITA Way

Challenges like these were not uncommon, and work often spilled over into ITA employees' personal lives. Chris Tessarowicz, the unofficial "voice" of InterVoice products, remembered getting a phone call at three in the morning from her husband, Mike, a Polish immigrant, and engineer Tuan Nguyen, a Vietnamese immigrant.

"They were trying to get some voice recognition ready to ship, and they were testing it, and it was not working. Mike realized, after testing it for I don't know how long, that no one could pronounce 'three' in an English manner," Chris said. "I jumped in a car, raced down, said 'three,' and it worked perfectly."[15]

Ultimately, the system was shipped before sunrise that day. Stories like this one are common among early employees. ITA was a fast-moving, fast-growing start-up company whose founders were directly involved, and the excitement level ran high. ITA operated on the fuel of opportunity.

"Whether there were six of us or twelve of us, we did whatever it took to get the job done—making the product, building the software, getting the computer ready, getting it into a box, typing the invoices, and getting it out the door," recalled Kathy Hackney, who became ITA's sixth employee in July 1984. Hackney had worked for Hammond at SD Systems and joined ITA as the office manager. "If we wanted four hundred letters out in the afternoon, Dan [Hammond] was in there stuffing envelopes, too. Everybody pitched in."[16]

Dwain Hammond, Dan's younger brother, became the eighth employee, signing on in December 1984 as an engineer. "There was a lot of camaraderie in the early years," he remembered. "We had a lot of good times. Over the years, the company has really become a home for a lot of us."[17]

ITA employees not only worked together, they also socialized with each other and were friends. It was the kind of company where employees remember partying in Dan Hammond's swimming pool, and stories abound about the holiday parties. On Halloween, employees were encouraged to come to work in costume, and Dan Hammond often judged the costume contest himself.

Although ITA amassed almost $1 million in its first year and enjoyed a seemingly limitless horizon of opportunity, its potential was still easy to

The Interactive Technology booth at the PCExpo show in September 1984. From left are Martin Durbeck; Dan Hammond; Mike Tessarowicz, cofounder and chairman; and Chris Tessarowicz, the first "voice" of InterVoice.

underestimate. When Hackney joined the company, she asked Hammond how big he thought it would get. He mused over the question for a moment, then guessed that ITA might someday hit twenty employees.[18]

The Troika Years

This might have been an easy mistake to make because ITA was still a company with a single customer. Obviously this was not a sustainable situation—once all the 7-Elevens had ITA systems, the business would dry up. Indeed, by late 1984, the Southland business was already starting to slow down. Then Hammond and Tessarowicz, however, made a fortunate connection. Durbeck introduced them to Al Fleener, a vice president of sales and marketing for Periphonics.[19] Originally, Durbeck thought Fleener might be a good customer, but it turned out that the sales executive had something else in mind.

Periphonics had just been purchased by Exxon, and Fleener was looking for something new. "I'd heard about Dan and Mike selling all these systems, and I met Mike somewhere," Fleener said. "I found out they had a talking board in a PC, and I said, 'Gee, I'd like to know more.'"[20]

He joined Interactive Technology Associates as an equal partner and executive vice president on January 7, 1985. Responsibilities were divided equally: Fleener, who had been selling computer systems to banks since the 1960s, focused on sales and marketing; Hammond handled operations and hardware engineering; and Tessarowicz focused on software engineering.

It didn't take long for Fleener to make his presence felt. "They weren't into sales and marketing," he remembered of his new partners. "They worked in blue jeans and shorts. It was like 'Build it, and they will come.'"[21]

Fleener, however, developed a three-pronged marketing approach for ITA's products: He believed they could be developed remotely, maintained remotely, and sold remotely. Later, ITA salespeople fondly recalled that Fleener even developed a videotape sales tool that he would send to prospective clients.

Fleener's more lasting contribution, however, was to push ITA toward a new market. He had considerable experience in banking, and he began to urge his partners to pursue the banking business. It seemed like a ripe industry because of the sheer volume of incoming calls that banks had to deal with. Before long, Fleener had identified five thousand potential customers in the banking industry, and ITA had signed up EDS and ITI as distributors.

The CallingCard

Obviously, ITA's Southland product, which allowed convenience store clerks to call a central database for a history of bad checks, was not exactly what banks needed. But ITA's engineers had been busy. In September 1984, at the PCExpo, the company showcased the first digital PBX peripheral based on an IBM PC. Originally called the PCX-800 and later renamed the CallingCard, it was an eight-port device that merged computer and phone operations with digital switching and voice capabilities.

Although it was never a commercial success as a PBX, the CallingCard represented a technological leap forward in almost every conceivable way. It allowed the PC to continue performing its usual data and word processing functions in the foreground while phone switching functions were controlled seamlessly in the background.[22]

With the CallingCard, it was possible to store digitized voice messages on the PC's internal hard drive and play them back as required. It could act as a normal telephone operator with on-line directory and phone status screens. It could compile a log of all phone calls by source, destination, duration, and time. It offered automatic transfer to voice mail instead of a no answer or busy signal. And it offered the proprietary ITA RobotOperator, which automatically processed and distributed incoming calls, using voice prompts and Touch-Tone technology, and routed them to saved digitized messages. The PCX-800 sold for less than $5,000 and plugged into the back of any standard PC. It was expandable to twelve lines and twenty extensions.

The RobotOperator

The CallingCard may not have sold commercially as a PBX, but it was a critical step forward. In the summer of 1985, ITA introduced the next generation of products built on the basic architecture of the CallingCard. Called the RobotOperator, the new product was a combination of proprietary hardware (CallingCard and VocalCard) and software (InterSoft) that provided telephone callers controlled access to information contained in a mainframe computer or internal database. It had a broad variety of applications. Banking customers, for example, no longer needed to wait for a human operator if they wanted to transfer funds, place a retail order, check market quotations, or open an IRA.

It was, in fact, the perfect product for the banking industry. Each system handled as many calls as necessary in modules of up to thirty-two lines, giving customers information without lengthy waits or busy signals. If a customer needed additional assistance, RobotOperator transferred calls to a human operator or agent.

Fleener later recalled the first RobotOperator sale, to Preston State Bank, in Dallas. At the time, many banks were skeptical of ITA's claim that most call-in customers were looking for something as simple as their account balance. But Fleener was adamant.

After our presentation, the president of the bank, Wendell Howell, went through a whole litany of why it wasn't any good. I said, "Let's do an experiment. You have six bookkeeping people on the phone nine to five every day. Let's have

THE FIRST TEN

ITA'S FIRST TEN EMPLOYEES WERE formally recognized in Christmas 1993 at InterVoice's employee Christmas Party and Ten Year Anniversary Celebration. The "First Ten" InterVoice employees, below, joined the company over a period of twenty months.

- Daniel D. Hammond, August 1983
- Michael H. Tessarowicz, August 1983
- Tuan K. Nguyen, August 1983
- Edwin A. Rivers, November 1983
- Rick L. Westcott, April 1984
- Kathy Y. Hackney, July 1984
- Donald B. Crosbie, September 1984
- Dwain H. Hammond, December 1984
- Alan D. Fleener, January 1985
- Marc A. Gardner, March 1985

The 1985 move to a new office, which at three thousand square feet was twice as large as the previous space. Tuan Nguyen was senior software engineer. Mike Tessarowicz is at right.

them tally what people are calling to ask." He agreed to that, and they tallied it, and 60 percent of the time, the first question was "What's my balance?" and about 90 percent of the time that was the second question.[23]

Howell next protested that his customers were "silk stocking" people who would object to talking to a robot operator. To allay this worry, Fleener arranged a demonstration at a party for the bank's most prestigious gold-standard accounts. At the party, all but one of the customers said they would be interested in the expanded service.

"Well," said Howell, "that settles it. I'll take it to the board."[24]

The bank ultimately bought two Robot-Operators, one as a backup. Incidentally, both

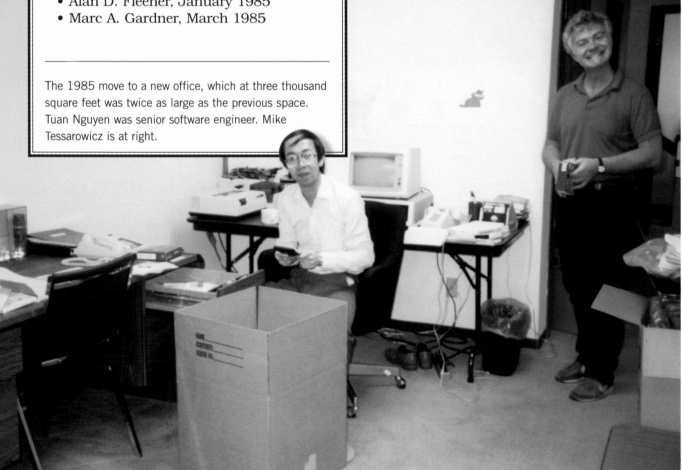

BORN TO TINKER

THE HAMMOND BROTHERS CAME FROM a family that took engineering seriously. As youngsters, Dan, Dwain, and Mac—who would all later work at InterVoice—took it for granted that their father was always working on

The Hammond children in 1964. Their father, William, was an engineer at Martin Marietta and a lifelong do-it-yourselfer. He built solar panels and air conditioners for the family home.

something in the garage. William Hammond was an aeronautical engineer at Martin Marietta, in Orlando, Florida, and he was well known for his penchant for "doing things himself."

"He took an air conditioning course, and when our air conditioning went out, he actually installed his own," recalled Dwain Hammond. "It was not something many people would attempt. I wouldn't recommend it either."[1]

Their father enjoyed tackling projects that other people would pay to have done or buy off the shelf. In the 1970s, when solar panels were popular, the senior Hammond built his own, putting a hot-water tank in the attic, soldering a panel together out of copper tubing, and installing it on the roof.

The women in the Hammond family were equally ambitious. Carol Hammond Knapp has three daughters and runs a private school in Orlando. Volina Hammond, who went back to school in her mid-30s after having four children, earned a degree in sociology and became a social worker with the city of Orlando. She graduated in the same class as her son Mac.

"It wasn't until I got older that I realized that what our mother did was pretty unusual," recalled Dwain Hammond.[2]

systems were destroyed within the year by fire and had to be replaced.

ITA Plans an Offering

In late 1984 and early 1985, ITA was in a state of transition. The company had done well its first year; it had posted revenues of slightly over $1 million because of the Southland sale, and it had introduced groundbreaking products as it tried to break into a new market. Yet it also continued to face challenges.

As ITA marketed aggressively to banks, it soon found out that, like Preston State Bank, most banks were notoriously conservative and fiercely resisted change. Although it seemed as if the RobotOperator would be an easy sell because its economics were so favorable, many banks resisted replacing their "human touch" with a machine. Similarly, many companies were used to seeing giant mainframes supporting IVR applications and had a hard time believing that ITA's PC and peripheral box could support their needs.

"There were some banks and other customer service organizations that did want it, to save money," remembered Marc Gardner, who joined the company as the tenth employee in 1985. "Then there were the ones who were dead set against it because they thought they would lose their personal touch—and they didn't like that."[25]

The challenge didn't end with the sale. Once banks were signed up, they often insisted on customized products. No two banks wanted the same script for callers, so ITA engineers spent a lot of time recording and coding personalized scripts for their bank customers.

As ITA worked through these issues, the company was also looking to finance its future growth. Among technology start-ups, cash is always an issue, especially when the company is moving products and investing in future research and development. ITA was no different.

While many of ITA's peers chose to approach banks or venture capitalists for seed money, Hammond and Tessarowicz had a different idea. At the 1984 PCExpo, where excited crowds waited to see the PCX-800, Hammond and Tessarowicz met an investment banker from D. H. Blair who wanted to do an initial public offering for ITA. By later standards, this might not seem so radical; throughout the 1990s, companies with negative revenue had massive public offerings on a regular basis. But in the mid-1980s, it was unheard of. ITA, with fewer than ten employees and revenues of about $1 million, seemed an unlikely candidate for such an early public offering.

The partners, however, got excited about a possible public offering and quickly wrote an optimistic business plan and sent it to D. H. Blair.

InterVoice

While the business plan was being studied, ITA continued to evolve. In February 1985, only a month after joining the company, Al Fleener was named chief operating officer (COO). Hammond was president, and Tessarowicz was chairman and CEO. Fleener, a stickler for trademarking and branding, soon involved the company in a discussion about its name. Interactive Technology Associates Incorporated was not the most attractive-sounding name, nor was it the most memorable. People often stumbled over it or abbreviated it. If ITA were really going public soon, it needed a different name.

The partners and the others soon realized they had already invented one memorable moniker:

InterVoice, the name of the programming language for the RobotOperator. People remembered InterVoice, and it had a nice ring to it. Thus in February 1985, the company name was officially changed to InterVoice.

"So that's how we got our name—although we were using it prior to that for our product," recalled Hammond.[26] To avoid confusion, ITA changed the name of its programming language to InterTalk.

A Powerful Partner

It was a busy time. Early employees recall the challenge of writing custom programs to satisfy new banking customers and struggling to maintain existing systems. Yet InterVoice remained a relatively tiny company, and its employees worked long hours, sometimes seven days a week.

"All of us did everything," Gardner remembered. "We did trade shows. We did sales support. We did development. We did sales. I'd say in the first three years in the company, you didn't really want to answer the phones on the weekends, if you were at home at all on the weekends, because you knew it was a customer calling and you might have to get on a plane."[27]

It was clear that the company faced an uphill climb. Although it had innovative technology, InterVoice used a platform, the IBM PC, that many smart business people still considered a toy. InterVoice customers were still leery of a small box that was supposed to do the same thing as much larger, more expensive systems. If it looked too good to be true, they reasoned, it probably was.

The situation was further complicated by the climate of the times. Throughout the early 1980s, phone equipment companies, technology companies, and computer whiz kids were popping up everywhere. Start-ups were a dime a dozen, and they fizzled with unsettling regularity. InterVoice's banking customers, on the other hand, prized stable, long-term vendors and had little appetite for risking their customer relationships on an unknown quantity.

Al Fleener recognized this roadblock and came up with a solution. Because InterVoice relied on IBM technology, it stood to reason that IBM might be interested in forming a partnership. Before long, InterVoice and Fleener struck a deal with IBM's banking division. As part of the deal, IBM demanded that InterVoice guarantee $1 million in PC purchases over the next year. "I said, 'No problem,'" Fleener remembered. "We were doing about $1 million at the time total, and the PC was 10 percent of our cost, so it was about $100,000. But I said no problem."[28]

In exchange, InterVoice got to put IBM's logo on its marketing material, thus glowing in the reflection of the giant's credibility. Later, IBM would use InterVoice's technology as the national beta test to see whether IBM technicians could service IBM PCs with "alien" equipment on the inside.

Tom Carter Joins the Board

Credibility with customers, although important, was only one challenge facing the company. As it prepared for the public offering, InterVoice knew it would soon come under the icy scrutiny of institutional investors and venture capitalists who wanted to know why they should invest in InterVoice. One of the banks underwriting the offering had, in fact, just demanded that InterVoice have a $400,000 backlog of orders before the offering could go through. Fortunately, Fleener landed a $250,000 contract with Empire Savings only a month before the scheduled public offering.

Hammond and Fleener also knew that outside investors would question the makeup of InterVoice's board. So far, the board of directors was entirely internal—InterVoice's management group had no outside oversight or advice.

In March 1985, the senior executives at InterVoice decided to add some high-octane power to their board, and Hammond already knew whom he wanted. Glancing through a trade journal, Fleener had seen the name of Tom Carter, the legendary figure whose Carterfone helped bring down AT&T's monopoly. Carter, a high-profile figure in the industry, would be a perfect candidate for an outside board member, and Fleener placed a call to him. "He was really brusque, but I told him what I wanted and what I thought he could do for us, and he said, 'Well, you come down here and see me,'" Fleener remembered.[29]

Fleener and Hammond soon hit the Texas highways and drove to Gun Barrel, Texas, where Carter owned a ranch. Gun Barrel was best known

as the home of an infamous woman who murdered several husbands and buried them under a well. When they met Carter, Hammond and Fleener asked him to join InterVoice's board. Carter agreed, although he would not formally join the board until just after InterVoice had gone public.

"Carter was a Texan's Texan," Hammond remembered. "He wore a cowboy hat, boots, and a bolo tie with turquoise in it. He wore that to every meeting he ever attended."[30]

Tessarowicz also remembered the famous Texan. "He was a mix of technology and back-country stuff," Tessarowicz said.

I remember when he came to look us over, and we were a very small company. I was there with Dwain and we were working on a board. Tom says, "Can you show me what you do?" So I turned it on and said it was a prototype, and as I was showing him some of the features, it caught on fire. He was very nice, and he said, "Maybe you guys need to spend some more time on this."[31]

InterVoice Goes Public

In April 1985, InterVoice moved to 1850 North Greenville Avenue, in Richardson. The new building, with three thousand square feet of office space, was like "hog heaven," remembered Hackney. "It was double the size."[32]

This new building had several offices, plus a lab area where Nguyen and Rivers worked, arranged in back-to-back suites. "Don Crosbie was the head of marketing when we moved into the Greenville facility," Rivers remembered.

He would sit across the hall from me, so I'd be sitting at my desk and he'd be talking to somebody on the phone saying "We can do this" and "We can do that," and I'd look at him and frown, like what are you talking about? So he'd say, "I'd better go check on that."[33]

Only a month after moving into the new building, the company made its first public offering, issuing 1.636 million shares of common stock. Before the offering, GTECH had owned about 20 percent of the company, with the rest split between

A TELCO LEGEND: TOM CARTER

TOM CARTER, THE MAN WHOSE Carterfone eventually opened up the telephone equipment and interconnect business, didn't want to pick a fight with AT&T.

In fact, at first, he tried to negotiate an agreement with the phone giant that would allow him to sell his two-way radio and connect it to a normal handset. AT&T refused his request, however, as it refused all others. Since the invention of the phone in the late nineteenth century, AT&T had allowed no foreign equipment to be hooked to its network. It owned the phones, the lines, and the service.

It wasn't until AT&T's refusal that Carter devoted himself wholeheartedly to defending his right to sell the Carterfone. The ensuing legal battle would cost Carter dearly. He lost his ranch as he converted his assets into capital and watched his business shrink from one hundred employees to one.

Those who knew Carter described him as a regular man with fierce determination. He couldn't abide the injustice he perceived—even if his victory would seem Pyrrhic. Yet it would not be an understatement to say that Tom Carter's dogged fight benefited every subsequent generation of consumer. Through his 1968 victory, he secured the right of independent companies to manufacture equipment and connect it to AT&T's previously protected telephone networks.

Soon after, MCI became the first private company to hook its long-distance network into local phone service, and a new industry was born. The AT&T monopoly officially crumbled in 1984.

After his victory, Carter remained active in the industry he helped create. In 1970, to establish a forum for other interconnects like himself, he started the North American Telephone Association, which was renamed the North American Telecommunications Association (NATA) in 1982. The original group was just seven people trying to sell and install telephone systems. Carter served as chairman and president of the association from 1970 to 1974 and was chairman emeritus at the time of his death on February 23, 1991, at age sixty-seven.

Carter's determination to create a free marketplace remains evident everywhere, in the form of fax machines, wireless modems, and other equipment we take for granted today. Even the Internet owes something to Tom Carter. Without the Carterfone decision, "users of the public switched network would not have been able to connect their computers and modems to the network, and the Internet would have been unlikely to develop," wrote Jason Oxman, counsel for advanced communications for the FCC's Office of Plans and Policy, in a 1999 paper.[1]

Hammond and Tessarowicz. After the offering, all three—GTECH, Hammond, and Tessarowicz— remained significant shareholders.

By the end of 1985, InterVoice had posted sales of more than $1 million. The figure was

Part of the InterVoice engineering and sales team standing outside the new headquarters building located at 1850 North Greenville Avenue, in Richardson. The company expanded rapidly from this location. From left are Marc Gardner, Rick Westcott, Tuan Nguyen, and Ed Rivers.

slightly down from the previous year, but it represented a substantial victory: in a single year, InterVoice had completely replaced the lost Southland revenue with sales to new banking customers. These first few years had witnessed a remarkable series of accomplishments for such a young company. It had landed a major contract with a national company, sold stock to the public, diversified into banking, and emblazoned its name in computer history as the first company in the world to use an IBM PC for voice applications. With so much success coming so fast, some of the challenges that face growing technology companies

were also surfacing. InterVoice was shipping so many systems that it couldn't divert resources to the issue of standards. New products were being developed on the fly, with new features added almost randomly.

"Every bank had a different computer," remembered Nguyen. "We were joking at the time that we had interfaced to every computer already because they were all different, and I spent a lot of time developing each of these interfaces."[34]

Dwain Hammond recalled that "there were a lot of challenges back then."

During the first five years, we were always working on ideas, trying to develop new interfaces for products. We never knew where our next deal was coming from, so we were trying everything. We were cranking out a lot of applications, and probably 25 percent had brand-new interfaces we had developed.[35]

Finally, and perhaps more importantly, the personal computer revolution had only just begun. The IBM PC, with its Intel 8080 processor, would be considered outdated in only two years as faster chips rolled out and IBM clones from companies like Hewlett-Packard and Compaq sprouted up all over the technological landscape.

InterVoice's role in the revolution—whether it was to lead or be swept aside—remained to be seen.

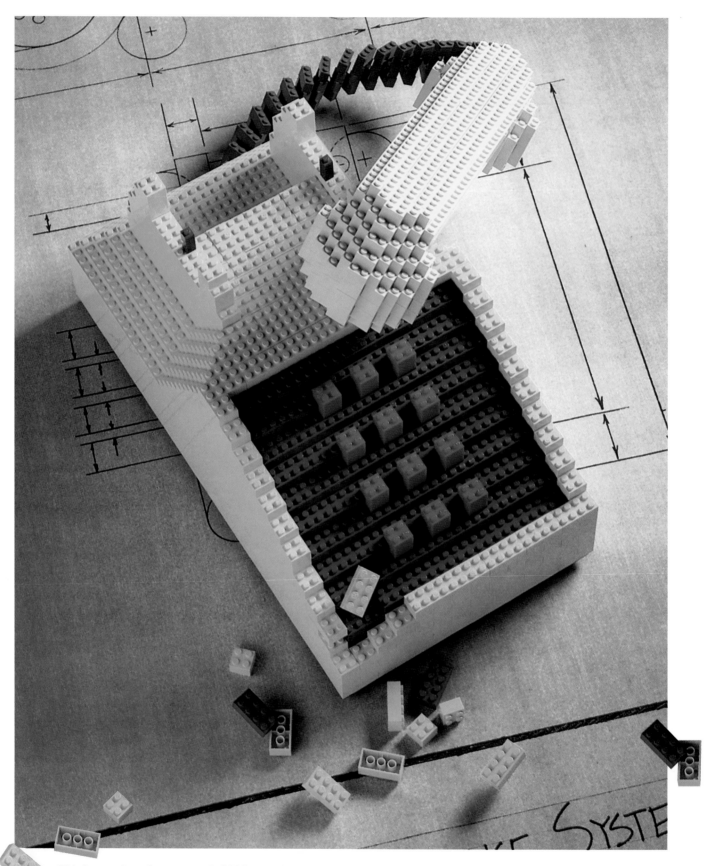

This image, from the company's 1990 annual report, illustrated the add-on functionality of the InterVoice system.

CHAPTER TWO

THE EARLY YEARS

1986–1990

*Customers grew to understand that once we turned it on and went
into production, it just ran. You wouldn't have any real problems with it.*

— Gordon Givens, on InterVoice products

Robot Operator™

IN 1986, DESPITE THE RAPID growth of the PC market, Inter-Voice still faced skepticism. Marc Gardner remembered installing an InterVoice system at EDS Credit Union to replace a Perception PDP 11 system. He walked into the data center with an IBM PC/XT under his arm and put it on the table, then went back for the monitor. When he said he had come to install the new system, the EDS manager said, "Well, let me open up the shipping dock. You can bring the truck around and unload the rest of it."[1]

When Gardner explained that the XT and monitor were the complete system, the manager "thought I was kidding. . . . So I plugged all the stuff in and brought up the communications with their host computer, and within a half hour, we were making calls through and getting data," Gardner recalled. The incredulous manager called all of his other coworkers over to see the "unbelievable" system.

Likewise, Keith Gyssler remembered banks' reluctance to sign on. He joined the company in 1986 and formed a "dynamic duo" with Al Fleener to pitch InterVoice products to banks. "When I joined, I remember thinking, 'What have I done?'" Gyssler said.

We weren't getting really warm receptions from the banks, which was our target market. They had

just installed ATMs, and they were trying to drive customers to ATMs. I remember a couple of people in those early sales calls saying, "We're not sure this technology is going to work because, frankly, we've already driven them out of the lobbies to ATMs, and here's another technology driving them out."[2]

A Bell Background

Reactions like this were not uncommon. The world still drew a clear distinction between telephone systems and computers. Moreover, if a computer were going to be involved in the phone system, the computer was likely to be a mainframe or a minicomputer. But things were changing quickly. InterVoice's early development took place against the backdrop of the biggest corporate breakup in American history.

In 1982, AT&T finally relented in its long-running antitrust suit with the Justice Department and agreed to break itself into pieces. The largest company in the world, one that had literally

---

The RobotOperator logo, featuring a graphic of a human operator with a slash drawn through her. The logo, a creation of Al Fleener, dramatically made its point.

invented telecommunications, was about to vanish. It would be replaced by a slimmed-down AT&T, owner of Western Electric and Bell Laboratories and purveyor of long distance, and twenty-two local phone companies known as RBOCs (Regional Bell Operating Companies).

AT&T could derive some solace from its break-up. The giant phone company would be allowed to enter the computer market. In 1956, in an interesting footnote to history, AT&T had agreed to stay out of the computer market in exchange for continued federal protection of its monopoly. Back then, company officers thought they had made a fool's bargain with the government—and they had come out on top. Things had changed so much by the time of the breakup, however, that AT&T Chairman Charlie

Brown remarked to the press, "No one contemplated twenty-five years ago that a revolution in modern technology would largely erase the difference between computer and communications."[3]

Yet that's exactly what was happening. The computer industry and the telephone industry were merging. Much later, industry wags would joke that if Alexander Graham Bell had been alive today, he would have invented a data network and put voice on top of it. Instead, in the 1980s, the business world was looking at the chaotic prospect of

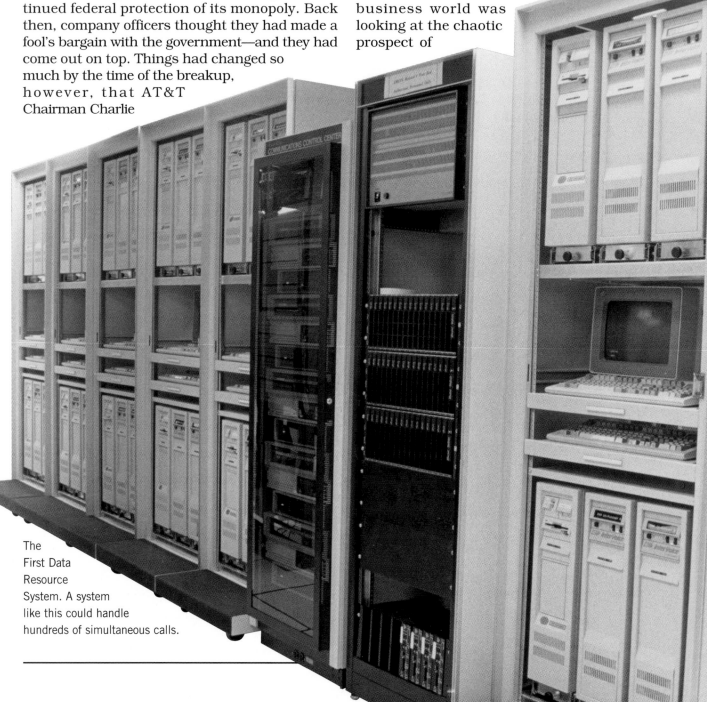

The First Data Resource System. A system like this could handle hundreds of simultaneous calls.

merging the established voice network with the emerging data network.

InterVoice, which was neither a true phone company nor a true computer company, bridged the gap between the two technologies with advanced voice technology.[4] It was a good place to be because the voice industry appeared to be on the brink of explosion. Voice systems were already appearing in PC systems for the general public. Texas Instruments, for example, offered voice options with its Professional series of PCs, and other vendors, such as Votan, had developed speech products geared towards the commercial segment of the industry.[5]

But InterVoice products had several advantages over most of the industry's other offerings. Because they were based on the IBM PC, InterVoice products were the most cost effective in every way: hardware, software, installation, and maintenance. Better yet—at least from InterVoice's perspective—the company didn't have to sink millions of dollars into research and development to develop better desktop systems. Instead, it relied on IBM and its many clone companies to introduce faster, more powerful hardware.

This strategy allowed InterVoice to put its energy into developing narrowly targeted voice products, many of which led the industry from a technical point of view. In 1986, InterVoice began working with Voice Control Systems (VCS) to develop VoiceDial, the first voice recognition on an interactive voice system.

Dan Hammond, Al Fleener, and VCS CEO Pete Foster held a press conference at the American Banking Association trade show, in New Orleans on May 11, 1986, to trumpet the new technology, which allowed a computer to recognize numbers spoken by a human voice.

"InterVoice was really the first company to use VCS technology in a commercial way," Foster later said.

We entered into a licensing agreement with InterVoice in 1985, and it was the first one for Voice Control Systems in the telecommunications area. InterVoice, by the licensing agreement, was the first one in the world to offer speech recognition in an interactive voice response system.[6]

This platform formed the backbone of InterVoice's voice-activated response systems for

Above: The InterVoice display at the American Banking Association trade show, in New Orleans in 1986. From left are Gary Strzinek, Don Crosbie, and Al Fleener.

Below: At the trade show, the company promoted its innovative voice response RobotOperator system as a cost-effective way for banks and other businesses to handle and route phone inquiries.

the next year and was later crucial in InterVoice's introduction into the European market.

Banking on Banks

Banks continued to be InterVoice's main customer, and the company continued pressing upstream against bank managers' biased views of machine operators, personal computers, and change in general. InterVoice, however, had a powerful argument for its products because the economics of the RobotOperator could not be equaled. A RobotOperator could handle four phone lines at once for a one-time price of $20,000, compared to $28,000 a year for a human operator.[7] The system didn't need sick days, vacation days, or benefits—and it could field customer calls twenty-four hours a day, seven days a week.[8] In fact, the RobotOperator's logo (which was not popular with everybody) featured the outline of a human operator with a bar drawn across her. The message was clear: no people.

These savings and the need for competitive customer service dominated the sales pitch Fleener designed for InterVoice. InterVoice salespeople soon discovered a fortunate character trait common in the banking industry: If one bank adopted a computerized phone data system, others wouldn't be far behind for fear of losing the race to offer better customer service. InterVoice also worked to expand its distribution network. By 1985, the company's direct sales channel and network of value-added resellers (VARs) boasted a customer base of approximately twenty-five hundred banks.

Above: First Alabama Bank, an InterVoice customer. Throughout the 1980s, the company made steady inroads into the banking industry, overcoming bankers' initial objections to machine operators.

Below left: The complete RobotOperator system. Because it was based on an IBM PC, the InterVoice system was a fraction of the size of competitive systems, leading many customers to initially wonder if the RobotOperator was up to the job.

Below right: A NationsBank call center in the 1980s. These call centers were expensive to maintain, and InterVoice's early sales pitch was based on the obvious economics of the labor-saving RobotOperator system.

"Just Do It"

Despite the challenges, InterVoice made inroads into the banking industry, and its success with its banking customers was reflected in its numbers. In 1986, revenues stood at $1.2 million, which was a slight improvement from the year before. By 1987, however, revenue grew to $3 million.

Along the way, InterVoice continued to deal with the varied demands of hundreds of banks. Every bank wanted a different interface, and

Above: California First Bank, another of InterVoice's customers. The company found that once one bank had signed on, its competitors would quickly follow.

Below: A RobotOperator system, left, and a Highboy RobotOperator. MCI used the powerful Highboy extensively.

InterVoice had not yet created standard development tools, so engineers had to travel extensively to troubleshoot installations around the country.

Myra Hambleton, who joined the company in 1987 as a software engineer, remembered being "pretty much thrown into whatever a customer might need." In fact, shortly after joining the company, she was sent to Honolulu,

Hawaii, for two weeks. Then she went immediately to Denmark, where she worked with a Dutch-speaking company to install a system whose specifications were in German. "I was over there by myself, but I didn't speak either language," Hambleton said. "We were really coding on the fly, and people ended up coming over from InterVoice join me."[9]

Engineers were often asked to fly around the country to service a series of customer sites. "We would put people where they were needed, and they really made a lot of sacrifices," said Gordon Givens, who joined the company as director of applications in the spring of 1987. In one case, Givens recalled, an engineer went out on what was supposed to be a three-day trip and came back six weeks later.

The Class of 1987

By this time, and despite the plateau in sales in 1987, InterVoice was adding people quickly, and roles within the company were changing. Al Fleener, who had joined as COO, executive vice president, and partner, became president in summer 1986, and Dan Hammond

InterVoice employees toast quarterly profits. InterVoice tended to surge forward quickly in revenue based on orders from large clients. Standing in front are Dan Hammond, left, and Al Fleener. Kathy Hackney is pictured center, and Marc Gardner is at the far right.

Inset: Gordon Givens, InterVoice's director of applications, joined the company in 1987 and later helped InterVoice move overseas.

became CEO. Tessarowicz continued as chairman. InterVoice also hired a group of people who would form the core of the company for the next fifteen years. Many of them were straight from college, had been recruited from Poland by Tessarowicz, or had worked at only one or two companies before joining InterVoice. Givens was charged with hiring a group of software developers fresh from college. This group included Myra Hambleton and Craig Evans and would become known as the Class of '87. At the same time, Tessarowicz recruited several engineers from Poland, including Bogdan Blaszczak, Walt

Mirkowicz, and Peter Koening. It was an exciting time to join InterVoice because the company was full of possibility.

Phil Walden, who had worked with Hammond a decade earlier at SD Systems, was also hired in 1987 and given the broad responsibility to develop the manufacturing organization. "The company had reached a point where it needed to be able to do something other than just build a few systems in R&D," Walden said.[10] At the time, when InterVoice got a new order, engineers would go to Sears and buy a single IBM PC and customize it back at the office. The whole process took at least two months.

By 1988, however, the manufacturing operation needed additional space. "So we set up an integration area," Walden remembered.

We built a chain-link fence inside the room, floor to ceiling, and we called it a stockroom. Then we actually purchased material so we'd have more material to integrate systems, and I think our second year, 1988, was pretty significant because a lot of pieces of the company, the selling side, the engineering side, customers, reliability of our products, and a whole lot of things, began to come together. We were growing very rapidly.[11]

In fact, almost every part of InterVoice felt growing pains. In the late 1980s, a host of departments coalesced, including the Applications Group, the Service Group, which sponsored the RealCare customer service program, the Documentation and Training Group, and many others.

Technology Advances

As InterVoice worked to streamline and grow, the R&D program continued to develop better products, usually in conjunction with new products from the computer industry. In April 1987, IBM announced the release of the Personal System/2 (PS/2) series of personal computers, which were twenty times faster than the IBM PC/XT, upon which the original RobotOperator was based. The new PC featured IBM's microchannel architecture, which offered InterVoice an opportunity to significantly increase the capabilities of its product line, providing feature-rich, user-active solutions for operator automation.

In response, InterVoice carried out a design project to combine IBM PS/2 power with a state-of-the-art, 25-megahertz digital signal processor (DSP) to provide flexible, software-controlled, telephone features. This project was put under the stewardship of Mike Polcyn, an engineer with DSP experience who joined the company in 1987 from Intecom.

InterVoice also trimmed labor-intensive tasks by inventing development tools so programmers could develop applications quickly. For example, InterGen, a high-level, nontechnical applications authoring tool, provided active control over RobotOperator's "conversation" with callers and computers.

A group of InterVoice employees in October 1987. From left are David Boyle, software engineer; Walt Mirkowicz, engineer; Barry Blackwelder, software engineer; Tuan Nguyen, software engineer; Rodney Ivester, engineer; Mike Polcyn, engineer; Phil Walden, vice president, manufacturing; Gene Gorka, engineer; John Clayton, engineer; Mickey Condray, engineer; Beverly Mitchell, sales secretary; Marjorie Fleener, sales; Peter Koening, engineer; and Craig Evans, software engineer.

At the same time, InterVoice also unveiled the fruit of its partnership with VCS. The VoiceDial enhancement to RobotOperator allowed callers without a Touch-Tone phone to "talk" to the computer. It was the first of its kind anywhere in the world.

The breakthrough technology would serve as the bridge that allowed InterVoice to successfully enter European markets, where Touch-Tone technology was relatively rare. Less than a year after introducing the new product, InterVoice signed Marconi Speech and Information Systems, a division of General Electric Company of the United Kingdom, as its first international distributor. Shortly after, the company signed Rockwell as a distributor and shipped its first products internationally. The first European InterVoice system was installed in Clydesdale Bank in England.

In 1987, InterVoice added DataConnect capabilities to the system, allowing a "caller" to access information through personal computer connections. DataConnect was especially valuable for managers preparing reports since RobotOperator could supply requested information, which could then be formatted or incorporated into existing documents.

The Ticker Talker

While no one doubted InterVoice's technological leadership, the company's sales effort still needed a boost. Toward this end, InterVoice began designing products for specific markets instead of developing products and seeking markets that might want them.

The outcome was a groundbreaking product, the VoiceQuote application for the RobotOperator, unveiled in 1988. Through the telephone, customers were able to access up-to-the-minute stock market information and create and store a representative "portfolio" for future inquiries.

Dan Hammond provided some perspective on the force that was driving these new applications in an article published in *Dallas/Fort Worth Technology Magazine* in November 1992:

> *There is clearly a driving requirement in the world today to provide more information to more people. More than ever, dissemination of information is crucial to good service. Not only are people calling to find their bank balances, but also they want to find the status of insurance claims, order items from catalogs, report electrical power outages, renew newspaper or magazine subscriptions, and register for university courses. Without voice automation, the cost of servicing these calls would become prohibitive.*[12]

Social Security Project

In 1989, InterVoice landed its largest installation yet. The company contracted to provide a multiprocessor system for the Rockwell Social Security project. The system was designed to allow recipients to call a toll-free number and answer a recorded questionnaire. The answers were recorded, then transcribed by human operators, and the recipients' concerns were addressed. It was the first installation in which InterVoice connected multiple systems.

As a system mandated by the government, the project needed to meet a specific deadline or the Social Security Administration would have to explain the delay to Congress.

Although it was a successful installation and product, the revenue it generated actually caused some headaches for the company. In 1989, revenue nearly doubled from $6 million the year before to $11 million. In 1990, it leaped to $20 million. In 1988, the *New York Times* listed InterVoice as the number-two gainer among all stock listed

The Richardson Chamber of Commerce dedicates the new InterVoice headquarters on Greenville Avenue. Dan Hammond and Don Crosbie are standing together, near the center right, both wearing ties.

on all exchanges, including NASDAQ, with an increase in stock price of 431 percent.

Although much of this spike was based on one client, it created expectations on Wall Street that InterVoice would continue growing by almost 100 percent every year—a growth rate that no company can maintain for long.

The Decade Ends

Heading toward 1990, InterVoice continued to do what it did best: introduce new and better products. In early 1989, it introduced RobotOperator/2, based on the VocalCard/2 and Fone Tower. By extending the maximum module size from thirty-two to seventy-two telephone lines, with virtually unlimited line support when connected to a LAN (local area network), it provided the most powerful and flexible voice response platform in the industry.

A significant enhancement introduced in the RobotOperator/2 system was T1 digital connectivity, allowing twenty-four phone conversations to take place simultaneously on a single line to the phone company. This capacity, along with ISDN-PRI (Integrated Systems Digital Network-Primary Rate Interface) support, allowed InterVoice systems to service large numbers of telephone lines on a single system more efficiently.[13]

InterVoice next announced a product direction called OneVoice, an integrated system approach that addressed all segments of the voice automation industry, including voice messaging, outbound call

processing, audiotex, call directing, and interactive voice response.

A Powerful Presence

In less than ten years, InterVoice had established itself as one of the top five players in an interactive voice response market that was expected to grow from $309 million in 1989 to $922 million in 1993.[14] By 1990, the company had organized itself into a number of key divisions, including client services and education, field services,

---

Above: After the Chamber of Commerce dedication, the InterVoice team celebrated in the new headquarters. From left are Barbie Boe; Don Crosbie, vice president, marketing; and Dan Hammond, CEO.

Below: An article from the *Dallas Morning News* in 1989. By this time, InterVoice was growing extremely rapidly, with revenue of $11 million. The company's stock was also hot, rising an astonishing 431 percent in 1988, making it the number two gainer on all stock indexes in the United States.

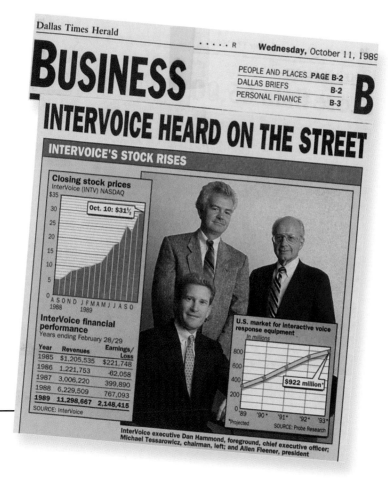

research and development, systems integration, sales and marketing, and administration.

InterVoice operated in a fiercely competitive marketplace that included firms such as AT&T, Syntellect, Periphonics, Votrax, and Perception Technology. In addition, manufacturers such as Dialogic produced personal computer add-in voice-processing boards for third parties and also integrated the boards with its own software to produce IVR systems.

By the end of the decade, InterVoice had sold more than nine hundred systems, or approximately eleven thousand lines, to more than five hundred end users, including Aetna, American Express, First Interstate Bancorp, J. C. Penney, MCI, National Data Corporation, National Westminsters Bank, the Social Security Administration, and Sprint. In addition to selling its products directly, it also sold to more than twenty resellers.

Gyssler, who had left the company in 1986 after six months, returned in 1989, as director of channel sales with responsibility for the resellers. For the Sprint sale, Gyssler remembered buying twenty Dallas Cowboy sweatshirts as giveaway gifts for the people at Sprint. Although Sprint was located in Kansas City, Dallas was a Super Bowl team that year.

A key to InterVoice's success was partnerships with companies such as EDS that sold a variety of computer services and equipment to financial institutions, according to Karl Kozarsky, an analyst with Probe Research. "They've developed one of the best distribution channels in a market that happens to be very hot right now," Kozarsky said.[15]

Because there were no patents or technological barriers to prevent other companies from manufacturing product configurations substantially similar to its own, InterVoice continued to com-

The original 1989 version of Fone Tower. The system relied on the IBM PS/2 and the InterVoice VocalCard/2. It was capable of offering digital network services.

pete primarily on product features, price, ease of use, availability, and reliability.

Corporate Growth

When InterVoice went public, with less than $1 million in revenue, it raised a few million dollars. As it turned out, however, the company was growing quickly enough that most of that money wasn't used right away. By 1989, however, InterVoice was ready to fund a major expansion with a secondary stock offering. On October 5, 1989, the company offered 1.5 million shares at $26 a share. The $40 million in proceeds was added to the $6.2 million cash already on hand.

At the 1989 annual meeting, shareholders approved proposals to elect eight people: Michael Tessarowicz, chairman of the board; Dan Hammond, chief executive officer, vice president-finance, treasurer, and director; Allen Fleener, president, chief operating officer, and director; Don Crosbie, vice president of marketing; Tom Carter, director; Joseph Pietropaolo, director; David Brandenburg, director; and William K. Woodruff, director. Of the new directors, David Brandenburg would play a pivotal role in the company's future.

InterVoice's stock continued to gain after the offering. Although it was near the $5 level in September 1988, by October 1989 it was trading above $30. That sixfold increase dwarfed the 40 percent increase the Dow Jones industrial average enjoyed during the same period.[16]

The money from the secondary offering went to work quickly. In December 1989, the company purchased new corporate facilities at 17811 Waterview Parkway, in Dallas, to house its 150 employees. The purchase of the five-story, seventy-five-thousand-square-foot building would prove cost effective from both an efficiency and an investment perspective.[17] During the initial move into the building, Dallas was besieged by an unusual freezing rain.

At the time, the space was much larger than management required, so the company

Above: The InterVoice open house in early 1990. From left are Don Crosbie, Mike Tessarowicz, Al Fleener, and Dan Hammond. This period of management would later be called the "troika" as Hammond, Tessarowicz, and Fleener grew InterVoice.

Right: Hammond, second from left, listens to Tom Carter, second from right. Carter was recruited to InterVoice's board because of both his importance in the interconnect industry and his name recognition.

leased space on the fourth floor to some psychiatrists. This proximity became a source of great amusement among employees. During times of stress, coworkers would often kid each other about the need to "grab a teddy bear and visit the fourth floor."

By January 1990, when InterVoice shipped its one-thousandth system, the company had achieved six years of solid growth. It had developed depth in the various technical disciplines used in its products, including voice and data communi-

cations, applications, system and device handler software, and on-line diagnostics and support.

But to continue to grow, InterVoice would need to shed its early "fly by the seat of your pants" mentality and develop additional organizational and operating skills. The company possessed the financial resources, personnel, plant facilities, and technical capabilities to continue to provide cutting-edge applications and services. Yet those resources would be tested to the utmost during the next decade when the company faced its first internal setbacks: the departure of two key executives and an agonizing race to shift its product base from DOS to IBM's new OS/2 operating system.

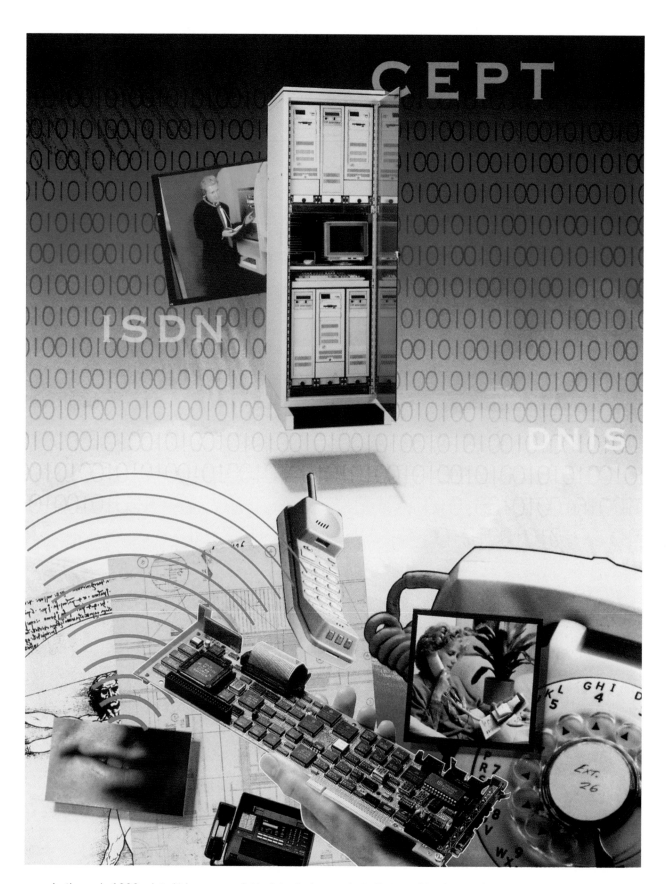

In the early 1990s, InterVoice grew quickly, introducing products that combined many functions on one platform.

CHAPTER THREE

INTERVOICE GROWS UP

1991–1994

We, me and Dan and Al, had the right combination of complementary things. . . . We were at the right time with the right product, and we worked very hard, but it was for a good purpose and for a good reason, and I'm proud that I was a part of it.

—Michael Tessarowicz, InterVoice cofounder

MOST OF THE EMPLOYEES WHO were around in the late 1980s cherish at least one favorite story of InterVoice going to extraordinary lengths to make a customer happy. Yet by early 1990 the company's sales had hit a plateau, and the growth rate had slowed. At the same time, the stock price began to drift downward. The problem certainly wasn't the lack of potential customers; thousands of banks still lacked InterVoice systems, and entire industries, including governments, had yet to adopt voice-activated systems.

Looking for a solution to the sales plateau, Al Fleener asked newly appointed director David Brandenburg to study the problem. Brandenburg was an electrical engineer and experienced entrepreneur who had just "retired" after selling his Dallas-based business, Entre Computer Centers. Fleener wanted Brandenburg to do a sales and marketing study for InterVoice and diagnose the situation.

"Al used to drive by our offices, and every time he would drive by, he would see my car there—mornings, nights, weekends, whenever it was," Brandenburg remembered. "He must have thought I worked hard. So I agreed to do the study. I didn't even really understand the company all that well, but as I learned more, I learned that we appeared to have a good market, but we were relatively

unknown, and we didn't have enough sales coverage. The main thing I suggested was that we hire more salespeople."[1]

In June 1990 the report was presented to the board, and subsequently Brandenburg was asked to join Inter-Voice as chief operating officer. In 1990, only six months into his early retirement, Brandenburg signed on. Later he would credit his wife, Diana, with providing the motivation for him to join the company by saying "He owed it to the company because he was on the board of directors."[2] Brandenburg signed a three-year employment contract.

Once on board, he found himself enveloped in InterVoice's stop-at-nothing approach to customer satisfaction. He remembered one time in particular when he and Dan Hammond and a few other people were on a conference call to a customer in Virginia who was having problems with software. Brandenburg and engineer Craig Evans agreed they would fly up there that night.

Because there were no flights into Richmond, the two flew into Washington, rented a car, and got

Dan Hammond in a Superman costume. Even as the company grew into a midsize corporation, Halloween was very popular at InterVoice, with costumes and a company-wide contest. Hammond often judged the contest himself.

to their hotel after midnight. The next day they drove to Richmond and pleaded with the manager to let them have more time and make it work.

The manager agreed, and the team went to work in the tiny closet where the InterVoice system was located. "We put Craig in there with a phone and locked the door, and he stayed there," Brandenburg said. "We didn't truly lock it, but he thought of it as being locked so he'd stay in there and get it done. He was in there about a week or so, working with the development staff [on the phone back in Texas], and finally got it working."[3]

Fortunately, InterVoice's systems were notoriously reliable. Once the engineers had one installed and running smoothly, it rarely developed difficulties. "Customers grew to understand that once we turned it on and went into production, it just ran," said Gordon Givens. "You wouldn't have any real problems with it."[4]

A Window on the World

InterVoice had earned this kind of stability because of its focus on superior technology. By the late 1980s and early 1990s, InterVoice and IBM shared a tradition of collaboration and cooperation. InterVoice had championed IBM's PC for business applications, and in return, IBM had given InterVoice some much-needed credibility.

So it seemed natural when IBM announced its new operating system in the late 1980s, OS/2, developed in conjunction with Microsoft, that InterVoice would be interested in switching to the new architecture.

"OS/2 was a much better operating system," remembered Michael Tessarowicz. "In itself, that wasn't a bad decision."[5]

It was, however, a gamble. By aligning itself so completely with IBM, InterVoice was betting that the OS/2 would become the standard operating system of the future. "We had identified OS/2 as the platform of the future because of the internal architecture, which was very well built for our purposes," remembered Walt Mirkowicz, a software engineer who had joined InterVoice in 1987.

But the ascendancy of OS/2 was a vision far from realized. In 1990, when OS/2 was already three years old, Microsoft announced its own proprietary operating system, called Windows 3.0. Soon afterward, IBM began offering Windows 3.0 as an option on its PS/2.

Because OS/2 was experiencing problems in the marketplace—it was buggy and required significantly more powerful computers than were available—Windows 3.0 was an immediate success. Before long, IBM's competitors began preloading Windows 3.0 on their machines, along with MS-DOS.[6]

By this time, however, InterVoice was already committed, both financially and emotionally, to OS/2.

The DOS-to-OS/2 Crisis

Switching operating systems, from DOS to OS/2, was a challenging task, and looking back, InterVoice CEO Dan Hammond would say it was a learning experience. In 1990, as David Brandenburg was still settling into his office, InterVoice began the enormous job of migrating its entire product base to the new operating system. Because OS/2 was a multitasking operating system, development changes were enormous, requiring new user interfaces, major rewrites on software, and development of new code.

Also, because the DOS system was more established, InterVoice programmers weren't able to include all the features on the new OS/2 platform.

A *Business Week* profile featuring the management troika of Al Fleener, Mike Tessarowicz, and Dan Hammond. By the early 1990s, after years of rapid growth and an initial public offering, InterVoice began to attract national media attention. *(Photo courtesy of Business Week.)*

A group of InterVoice senior executives in 1991. From left are David Brandenburg, Don Crosbie, Al Fleener, and Dan Hammond. It was a particularly tough year as the company struggled to migrate its product platform to OS/2.

"When you start over," remarked programmer Myra Hambleton, "you've got to give yourself some time. Number one, you've got to get it working, and number two, you've got to build features on top of it."[7]

InterVoice programmers had to learn a new development system at the same time they were updating the old software for existing customers. This task was complicated by the relative newness of the OS/2 operating system. Because it was new, it was difficult to determine whether a bug was in the OS/2 platform or the InterVoice system. In many cases, InterVoice had to deliver DOS initially and promise to give free upgrades when the OS/2 system was finished.

Worst of all, once the systems were in the field, they crashed regularly, losing features that had to be built back in as upgrades were made to hardware. Craig Evans, an engineer who had once spent two weeks "locked in a closet" during a tough installation, clearly remembered the first OS/2 installation, which was for the state of Virginia. "I went up with David [Brandenburg], and things were difficult when we got there, and he bought us some time," Evans said.

We worked over the period of a week or two but had not quite gotten to where we needed to be, and the customer had given up and said, "We can't go forward with this," to put it mildly. I remember David flying back to Virginia and me thinking he was just wasting his time. At that time, I would have bet anything, all the money I had, that they weren't going to listen to him. I remember sitting in an office with David and the senior management person for Virginia, and I just watched him work with this guy and buy us another chance. We were able to work through our issues and make it a success.[8]

As the stakes climbed, InterVoice went into crisis mode. Dan Hammond placed a call to the heads of hardware and software engineering and said, "Guys, we're going down the tubes if you can't make this software work." He recalled that "we set up a war room, and the engineers camped in there for a month. David Brandenburg and I were flying out weekly, talking to customers who were ready to throw us out."[9]

During the OS/2 switchover, research and development (R&D) expenses, typically around 10 percent of InterVoice's budget, shot up to 17 percent. This intense and stressful period was later described by company veterans as the "years of the eighty-hour workweek." "We canceled a lot of vacations. It was a tough year," recalled engineer Marc Gardner.[10]

The development challenges were compounded by miscommunication between InterVoice engineers and the sales force. Before the OS/2 product was completely ready, the sales force began talking it up—describing its advantages over the DOS version and preparing customers for it. In the short run, this publicity had the effect of postponing purchases. Then, when the OS/2 product was delivered, customers were often angry because it did not live up to their expectations.

"Everybody was out there selling the future because we had a robust platform," remembered salesman Keith Gyssler. "It could do a lot of things. But it didn't necessarily do them right this minute. So consequently, we would always be out in front of ourselves in terms of what we were selling, and that would get us into a whole other set of problems."[11] To bring the sales effort more in line with the reality, the company developed a concept called SWAT for Sell What's Available Today.

Despite the challenges involved, both IBM and InterVoice continued to invest in the new architecture. In 1992, IBM launched OS/2 2.0, a completely redesigned, rewritten system with a graphical interface, stable DOS program compatibility, and Windows program capability. It was a strong operating system designed to compete with the ever more dominant Microsoft Windows operating system. By this time, IBM had taken over development of OS/2 because it felt that Microsoft was directing too many resources to Windows at the expense of OS/2.

Over the next two years, IBM programmers continued to improve the system, adding features and fixing the mountain of bugs that appeared in the initial releases. OS/2 sales were steadily increasing —but never kept pace with Windows sales because Windows came preloaded on almost every computer sold in the United States.[12]

By 1992, InterVoice's switch to OS/2 was basically complete, and the episode began to fade into corporate history. Before long, however, the company would again switch architectures, this time to a Windows NT platform. Fortunately, that transition would be much smoother.

The Troika Breaks Up

In the midst of switching to a new operating system, InterVoice was also dealing with a more familiar problem: cycles of stellar years followed by a sales plateau. For the most part, this pattern was driven by its huge clients. The Southland deal, for example, was followed by flat revenue for a year. In 1991, InterVoice faced another period of flat sales after the gigantic Rockwell project wrapped up. Sales that year remained at $20 million.

At the same time, while dealing with the change to OS/2, InterVoice was undergoing internal changes. David Brandenburg had signed on with the company for three years as chief operating officer in June 1990.[13] His ascension coincided with the planned departure of two of InterVoice's longtime leaders. By May 1990, InterVoice founder Mike Tessarowicz had already ceased his day-to-day involvement. The reasons were varied, but no hard feelings intruded between him and the company he helped create. Ever the entrepreneur, he left InterVoice in December 1990 to found another technology company, called GTESS. Tuan Nguyen, the Vietnamese engineer recruited by Tessarowicz, would eventually join him.

Al Fleener, the third leg of the management troika, was also preparing to leave. Fleener, who had introduced the company to the banking industry and was still heading up the sales and marketing function, announced his retirement for the end of 1991. Another dyed-in-the-wool entrepreneur, Fleener left InterVoice to pursue a career in financing public corporations, eventually starting his own venture capital firm. "This was the third company I'd been involved with, and I liked financing companies," Fleener remembered, "I just felt it was a good time."[14]

His seat on the board was filled by George Platt Sr., the third outside director, joining Bill Woodruff and Joe Pietropaolo.

With these two seats empty, InterVoice relied on known quantities. Effective January 1, 1991, Dan Hammond was unanimously elected chairman of the board to fill Tessarowicz's empty seat,

A company family picnic and bingo party in 1992. Although InterVoice was already too large and growing too fast to maintain its intensely family-like culture, it was still a very friendly company with low turnover.

and he retained the title of CEO. In July, in conjunction with Fleener's departure, Bradenburg was named president of InterVoice.

A New Team Forms

With Brandenburg promoted to a senior operating role and Fleener and Tessarowicz gone, InterVoice was clearly in a state of transition. "It became obvious we needed a different management structure to grow the company," Dan Hammond later said. "We needed to delegate. We needed to enable the organization to grow, and that's when we started creating what David Brandenburg called a professionally managed organization."[15]

The first hole to fill was in the sales and marketing side of InterVoice. George Platt recommended a sales expert named Mike Barker, vice president of sales at DSC Communications Corporation. Barker was perfectly suited for the job. He had eighteen years of experience in the telecommunications and computer industries, even building a large PBX sales organization for Rolm. Just as Al Fleener had moved InterVoice into banking, Barker would be able to introduce InterVoice products to the telecommunications industry. In 1991, he joined InterVoice as senior vice president, sales and marketing.

"I liked what I saw," Barker later said. "I liked the size of the company because of the ability to get things done. I felt like I could influence the company's success."[16]

Like Brandenburg before him, Barker recommended that InterVoice rapidly scale up its sales effort.

"When I came on board, they had six salespeople, and they were all great guys and gals," Barker remembered. "They were very young, but energetic and very smart. But InterVoice was underspending in sales, like a lot of companies do. We immediately doubled the number of salespeople."[17]

To train the new people, Barker's team drew up a sales training plan and instituted quarterly meetings to update the sales staff on new products. These meetings were particularly helpful in the wake of the OS/2 issue and the miscommunication between engineering and the sales force that had caused salespeople to hype a product before it was ready. Within a year, the sales and engineering groups were participating in Barker-sponsored teambuilding exercises to increase communication.

Barker also founded an engineering support organization. Until that time, if a customer had a problem or question that the salesperson could not answer, an InterVoice engineer was called out of the development department. "It was disruptive to engineering," Barker remembered, "and they hated it. So we found a couple people in the engineering group who wanted to come into sales engineering."[18]

One of these engineers was Mike Polcyn, a development engineer who was named sales engineering manager. From then on, Polcyn and his department bridged the gap between the engineering department and the sales department.

"He was perfect," Barker later said. "He leveraged our salespeople immediately because they were able to have someone to go to, or go with them to calls. Customers will believe a salesperson to a certain point, but it was great to have Mike there to give that level of credibility that you needed to close the business."[19]

Around the same time Barker came on, other executives were moving into position, forming a core of professional managers who each championed the development of formal processes and structures in their respective organizations. In 1992 Rob-Roy Graham was hired as controller. Two years later, he would be named chief financial officer in conjunction with the retirement of Don Crosbie, the missionary turned salesman turned finance expert.

In the legal area, Dean Howell joined the company in 1992 as corporate counsel. He was the first in-house lawyer at InterVoice; before he joined the company, InterVoice had used a local firm for outside counsel. David Tannenbaum, one of the attorneys with the Dallas firm Fulbright & Jaworski, represented InterVoice in its pursuit of intellectual property protection. He helped build the "wall of patents" protecting InterVoice products. "Dan Hammond had the vision early on that if you have a lot patents, it's less likely anyone will want to bring a lawsuit against you," Tannenbaum said. "I had the honor of writing the first patent." These patents, dozens in all, would eventually hang on a wall at InterVoice, tracing a time line through the technology highlights and managerial development of the company.

Howell remembered that a "big part" of his job was to continue Tannenbaum's aggressive patent program and formalize it.

"We worked with Tannenbaum to come up with a plan," Howell said. "Skip Cave worked with the engineering group to make sure they knew about the program and they were aware that we have awards that we give to people in the company when they come up with ideas that are patented."[20]

The manufacturing department, too, underwent a formalization under Phil Walden, who had been with InterVoice for several years. In 1991 the product cycle was still about thirty days, but Dan Hammond pressed Walden to cut it in half.

"Around this time, I went on a tour of Tandem, which made very big, complicated computers," Walden said. "At one point in the tour, the guide asked a lady in the shop how long it took to build a computer, and I was blown away. From the time it went on the production line until it was in testing and ready to ship was three days. I said, 'Excuse me? I can't even build this little box with some boards in it and load software in less than thirty days. And my boss wants me to do it in two weeks.'"[21]

Walden began to study the company's processes and noticed its extensive planning system. "So I came back to Dallas, and I thought about this for a long time," he said.

I realized I had to completely redesign and overhaul the entire manufacturing organization. We changed our processes. We changed people. We changed the organization. We planned differently. Part of it had to do with providing some inventory. Part of it had to do with working more closely with sales and order-entry people to understand what they wanted. Some of it had to do with standardizing our product. Some of it had to do with documenting and identifying things so we did not have so many variables. The result is that, within eighteen months, we were able to get manufacturing time down not only to two weeks, but to a consistent one week.[22]

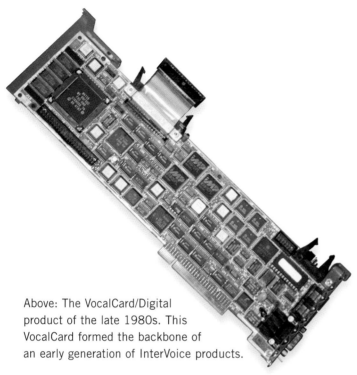

Above: The VocalCard/Digital product of the late 1980s. This VocalCard formed the backbone of an early generation of InterVoice products.

Below: Dan Hammond celebrating his fortieth birthday. With David Brandenburg as president, Hammond and InterVoice began to recruit a new class of seasoned professionals in the early 1990s to grow the company.

This maturation process—adding professional managers, formalizing procedures, and making rules—is not uncommon in fast-growing, entrepreneurial companies, but InterVoice stands out because of Dan Hammond's continuing daily involvement. Many engineers who create products that create companies begin to feel constricted after their brainchild grows to a certain point, and InterVoice in 1992 was certainly at that point. It had 258 employees and revenues of $30 million. It was clearly not a company whose employees hung out at the CEO's house and saw each other socially on weekends. Moreover, one of the founders had already left to pursue other ventures.

Yet Hammond seemed to thrive on the growth, and many InterVoice observers would later remark upon how excited he seemed and how hard he worked to learn the skills necessary to transform himself from a development engineer into the CEO of a multi-million-dollar, global technology company.

Joe Pietropaolo, a financial executive at GTECH, joined the InterVoice board in 1989 and remained on the board into 2002. "It was incredible to watch Dan Hammond mature as a manager," Pietropaolo said in 2001.

> Dan was a techie, and the technology person can get away with running the company for a while, but normally it doesn't last too long because they don't have other good management skills. But Dan really brought himself forward.
>
> At the beginning, Dan didn't have too much patience for numbers and management skills and techniques. He was concerned with development of products and technology. But fifteen years later, it was pretty much 180 degrees. He was very skillful at dealing with people, very good at recruiting people. He had a good working knowledge of the numbers and was also able to operate the company.[23]

Speaking with OneVoice

By November 1992, with the OS/2 crisis fading and a new team of seasoned managers in place, InterVoice was back on track. It was now the clear market leader, with about ten percent of a highly fragmented, $400 million market that was growing at 40 percent annually, according to some analysts.[24] In 1993, the company posted revenues of $45 million. That figure would almost double in two years.

This remarkable performance was partly a reflection of InterVoice's growing share of the expanding voice processing market, which was predicted to reach nearly $1.1 billion in the U.S. by 1995—a growth of 600 percent in six years. Experts also forecast that the international market for voice processing would begin doubling every year for the next several years.[25]

InterVoice planned to remain the technology leader. In the early 1990s, the engineering and development group, run by Dwain Hammond and a software engineer named Eric Weeren, was working on a new OS/2-based product called One-Voice. The new system represented another leap forward in voice technology. Not only could it "talk" to any of the other IBM operating systems, it was the first to combine five highly sought-after functions: automated call processing, voice mail, audiotex, outbound call processing, and interactive voice response.[26]

InterVoice management believed that OneVoice would be attractive to companies in a wide variety of industries—from computer and switch manufacturers to large enterprises—because it was compatible with their strategic direction and based on industry standards. OneVoice was based on several core elements, including IBM's PS/2, OS/2, and MicroChannel architecture, coupled with the proprietary InterVoice VoiceChannel architecture.

The versatile MicroChannel card provided a full twenty-four-channeled digital T1 connection to the telephone company in the United States; in Europe it provided thirty channels and was compatible with E1 standards.

The beauty of the InterVoice VoiceChannel architecture, though, was that it provided for additional functionality without disturbing the base platform through the use of shared resource cards. The shared resource card had a number of digital signal processors (DSPs), which allowed InterVoice to load software features as they emerged without affecting the base platform. In essence, InterVoice could create a never ending flow of features and functions to the software: voice recognition, text to speech, hearing-impaired modem, multiline fax capabilities—whatever the technology allowed.[27]

This platform would form the backbone of InterVoice products for the next decade. Later products such as OneVoice PCS would consolidate office, home, cellular, fax, and pager into a single number, while Agent Connect would offer call switching and simultaneous data transmission over the OneVoice/Call Center platform. Within two years, InterVoice would offer voice-activated dialing.[28]

Voice Takes Over

By this time, the United States was firmly entrenched in what would later be dubbed the "Information Age." The manifestations of this new age were everywhere, and InterVoice technology was at the vanguard. Organizations were turning increasingly to automation to hold down costs.[29]

"It wasn't a hard sell," said Mike Barker. "It was an easy story to show the person who was making the decision that there is a huge payoff. The systems often paid for themselves in six months."[30]

The InterVoice management in 1993. That year, the company posted revenue of $45 million and broke ground for a larger headquarters building. With the voice automation industry poised to explode, InterVoice revenues would double over the next year.

Yet with this increased opportunity came increased responsibility. It was no longer enough for a company to simply purchase a voice automation system to increase productivity. Corporations were now demanding that the voice automation piece of their architecture fit in with their IT operating systems and networks. Barker observed that the "water might look three feet deep, but it's actually thirty feet deep."[31]

In 1992, Hammond told the *Wall Street Transcript*, "I have observed a transition from a short-term, tactical view of solving specific problems at a specific period in time, to looking for a solution that will address the near-term requirements and also longer-term issues so that this piece of equipment fits and is controllable from their network control center."[32]

As the target industries multiplied, distribution became an issue. It was no longer enough to have an Al Fleener moving the company into banking or a Mike Barker pushing InterVoice toward telecommunications. The company needed a deep distribution system that could reach the whole spectrum of American industry, addressing each segment.

The voice automation field was generally viewed in terms of four market segments: voice mail, dominated by Octel, VMX, and switch companies including Rolm, AT&T, and Northern Telecom; interactive voice response (IVR), which InterVoice dominated; audiotex, which companies such as Brite Voice were strong in; and outbound call processing, which included key players such as Davox, Digital Systems, Melita, and several others.[33]

Although each of the companies in those segments viewed all of the others as targets—because the platforms each possessed could address the other areas of voice automation—the distribution required to move from one segment to another was different. The distribution to the IVR market was particularly difficult because the product had a customization level and required expertise in several different technological areas.

Like the others, InterVoice scrambled to leverage its product through as many distribution channels as possible. "The challenge that we face is having a platform that is broad and has enough capabilities to serve those four segments," Hammond said. "I don't think any of our competitors has the platform

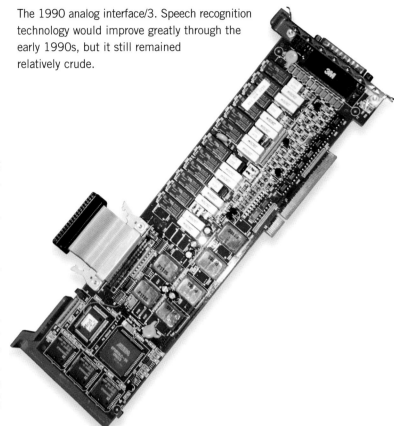

The 1990 analog interface/3. Speech recognition technology would improve greatly through the early 1990s, but it still remained relatively crude.

to enable them to move across the different segments of the industry as easily as we can."[34]

At the same time, two important areas of voice recognition, automatic speech recognition (ASR), which enabled people to give verbal commands to machines, and text-to-speech technology (TTS) continued to advance. The market research firm Voice Information Associates estimated that the market for speech recognition would grow to $751 million in 1997 from $189 million in 1992, while the text-to-speech business would grow in end-user market revenue to $535 million in 1997.[35]

While speech recognition technology was rapidly improving in its ability to recognize spoken digits and key words, it remained limited for a variety of reasons. Machines might not recognize different accents or pronunciations, and vocabulary was always an issue. Even into the mid-1990s, most voice-activated response systems understood relatively few words.

"It had to be speaker independent," said Skip Cave, an engineer who had worked with InterVoice since its founding and joined the company in 1989.

That means you could have anyone say "one" and you still had to recognize it, whether it was a southern accent or a Boston accent. That was the first stage. From there, we would start pushing for lots of other things. We'd like to be able to recognize characters, too, and that was tough. Then the next generation would be the single-word recognition, where you could ask a customer something like "Would you like your balance or last five checks?" The customer would answer "balance" or "last five checks."[36]

An International Presence

This steady evolution of technology benefited users not just in the United States. In fact, the development of speech-recognition technology opened up the entire IVR market in Europe, where Touch-Tone was not as prevalent as in the United States. This trend, coupled with the steady privatization of the European telecommunications system, presented tremendous opportunity to Inter-Voice. Between 1980, when the United Kingdom privatized British Telecom, and 1998, when the entire continent deregulated, Europe underwent a massive transformation in its telecommunications market, one that was similar in effect the breakup of AT&T.[37]

As countries such as Germany and France headed toward privatization and European countries began to deploy voice technologies for use as

A gathering of executives from Siemens and InterVoice in late 1993, celebrating the two companies' impending distributorship agreement. Dan Hammond and Werner Schmuking, chairman and CEO of Siemens, are seated.

Below: David Christal, former vice president of InterVoice S.A., Paris. He was the company's first international sales executive.

audiotex systems, interest in integrated platforms that could handle IVR, predictive dialing, and other technologies grew.

In January 1991, hoping to exploit this rapidly growing market, InterVoice established a European subsidiary in Paris and set up a series of agreements with European resellers to move InterVoice products across the Continent. The operation was set up and staffed by InterVoice executive Louis Bonét.

The Paris office seemed to be an early success story. In the first year, remembered Rob-Roy Graham, the office "saw a dramatic rise in revenue," but for an unexpected and unwelcome reason. "Company officers discovered to their chagrin that our products had been adapted and

sold by our distributors to corner the market for audio sex," Graham remembered. "Obviously, when the governments took a dim view of that kind of behavior, our business went down rather dramatically."[38]

The loss of this business didn't have any permanent effect on the growing European market, however. International sales as a percentage of total sales grew from 8 percent in 1990 to 11 percent in 1991 and to 16 percent in 1992. By April 1993, the company had established an office in Singapore and began building Pacific Rim distribution.

"We started with a few distributors over there," Givens said. "I remember doing a whirlwind tour through the Pacific Rim. I think I did twenty-five thousand miles in twenty-two days. We went from

Tokyo to Singapore to Australia to New Zealand, then back to Singapore and on to Hong Kong and Bangkok."[39]

That effort paid off handsomely by the end of 1994 with the doubling of Pacific Rim sales.[40]

InterVoice also expanded sales in Latin America through installation of the first multiport fax application at the largest bank in Venezuela. A major company in Chile placed an order for the InterVoice OneVoice/Message Center, marking the first international sale of that application.

Through its European subsidiary, InterVoice S.A., InterVoice continued to penetrate new geographical markets, adding Finland and Switzerland to the list in 1994, for a total of twenty-seven countries throughout Europe, the Middle East, and Africa. The sales and technical staff expanded to accommodate the new business, and major emphasis was placed on widening activities in Germany, France, Italy, and the United Kingdom.[41]

By 1994, InterVoice had installed more than 3,950 systems in more than forty countries. It had begun to establish itself as a global leader in interactive information response throughout the Pacific

Dan Hammond, left, watches as Werner Schmuking signs the distribution agreement between InterVoice and Siemens in late 1994. This relationship yielded major benefits through the rest of the decade.

Rim, Europe, the Middle East, North America, and Central and South America. Its speech recognition technology was available in thirty-six languages, including Russian, Cantonese, and Vietnamese.[42]

International expansion continued with the signing of Telecom Equipment Pte Ltd. as the InterVoice distributor in Singapore, Malaysia, and Brunei in January 1994. Another important agreement was signed in September 1994 when Siemens Private Communications Systems Group agreed to distribute InterVoice's automated call processing solutions in Europe. Siemens was a world leader in private telecommunications systems, with annual sales of $4.2 billion, more than 450,000 customers, and 900,000 systems installed worldwide.

Finally, in late 1995, InterVoice signed a three-year purchase agreement with a western Europe–based global provider of communications equipment and services. In Latin America, business doubled in 1995 over the previous year, fueled by sales in Argentina, Venezuela, and Mexico. InterVoice also further expanded distribution channels in Asia, adding distributors in Singapore, Thailand, India, and Malaysia.[43]

A NASDAQ Roller Coaster

InterVoice's stock history was like its sales history: volatile. During the worst of the OS/2 crisis in 1990, one Friday the thirteenth proved an unlucky day for InterVoice stock as management watched it dive to $12.75. The company ended the week down almost $6.[44]

The stock also suffered from that year's first-quarter report, in which InterVoice posted a profit of $1.19 million on sales of $4.87 million—figures roughly comparable to the same period the year before, but still below expectations. Other factors contributing to the stock drop were a falloff in orders from value-added resellers and an under-investment in the sales function.

Opposite: Telecommunications turned out to be a major market for InterVoice throughout the 1990s. The company built enterprise systems that were sold to telecommunications companies like MCI, GTE, and many others.

The bright side for InterVoice, industry observers noted, was that the demand for its products would be healthy for some time to come. "If you had to say it in a line, it would be, 'Watch these guys. A year from now, they'll be back,'" Erik Jansen, an analyst with the Robertson, Stephens & Co. investment banking firm, said.[45]

By 1993, the stock had recovered, closing at $21.75 on September 27, 1993, having risen from a low of $6.8125 in January.[46] The January "crater," in fact, would help convince David Brandenburg, then the company president, to extend his three-year employment contract for another year or so, until the stock price recovered.[47]

During the 1990s, InterVoice stock would split three times: October 16, 1992; August 16, 1993; and January 20, 1999.[48]

A Taste of the Telco Biz

In 1993, InterVoice signed a large order with MCI Telecommunications to help the phone giant create a national 1-800-COLLECT system. Bogdan Blaszczak, a software engineer who joined InterVoice in 1988, remembered the intensity of the project. "It took two years before we started talking about the completion of that project," Blaszczak said. "It got to the point of having daily conference calls with MCI."[49]

Because of the giant MCI order, sales to the telecommunications market, primarily to MCI, contributed 36 percent to the company's domestic sales growth in 1994.[50]

"It was great business," remembered Dwain Hammond. "After that, we said, 'We have to figure out how to get more of these kinds of deals,' and we probably put two-thirds of the focus in R&D on going after the telecom deals."[51] In February 1994, InterVoice announced the release of OneVoice Network Solutions for telco applications.

Over that year, InterVoice's telco channel business grew to clients such as GTE, LDDS, CANTV, and U.S. West's wireless operation. The company was also taking the first step in establishing synergy between CPE and telco products, positioning itself as a leading supplier to Regional Bell Operating Companies (RBOCs) and other telcos in the network-based IVR market as it continued to evolve.[52]

To further bolster its telecommunications business, InterVoice announced the acquisition of

The company's headquarters expansion at 17811 Waterview Parkway under construction. The earlier headquarters stands to the right of the new construction.

Opposite: In inset at left, Don Crosbie addresses the crowd at the ground breaking for the new facility. In inset at right, the ceremonial first shovelfuls are thrown out. With shovels, from left, are David Brandenburg; Florence Shapiro, state senator; Steve Bartlett, Dallas mayor; Helen Carter, Tom Carter's widow; and Dan Hammond.

VoicePlex Corporation in August 1994 for $8 million in cash and 225,000 shares of InterVoice common stock. VoicePlex, a Dallas-based company with about twenty-five employees, developed and sold UNIX-based voice-processing systems for telcos.

This acquisition, which was negotiated by David Brandenburg, was InterVoice's first corporate acquisition and one of its first moves toward network systems. "We found that most telcos wanted a UNIX-based system instead of an OS/2 system," said Dan Hammond.[53]

The Carter Building

In September 1993, InterVoice, which had once again outgrown its headquarters, broke ground on what would become known as the Carter Building in honor of Tom Carter, who had died in 1991.

By the following summer, many R&D and manufacturing and systems integration departments had relocated into approximately 90,000 square feet of the new space. By July 1994, the 150,000-square-foot facility was completed, expanding InterVoice's headquarters complex to a total of 225,000 square feet. Like earlier headquarters, the Waterview Parkway location would be a wise long-term investment. According to controller Graham, InterVoice expected its buildings "to yield a significant amount of cash."[54]

Shortly after the expansion, the company celebrated its tenth anniversary. It was a proud moment. Almost seven hundred guests attended the Christmas party and ten-year celebration. Some of the highlights included a special "InterVoice Network News" presentation, a mockumentary that featured candid interviews with InterVoice employees. InterVoice's "First Ten" employees were presented with plaques celebrating their various achievements.

Throughout its anniversary year, the executive makeup of the company continued its transformation. In March 1994, Mike Barker was named COO of InterVoice, then promoted to president and COO in September. With his promotion, Barker was taking over from David Brandenburg, who by 1994 wanted to begin phasing out of InterVoice management. In late 1994, Brandenburg assumed the role of vice chairman, an oversight

INTERVOICE'S TEN YEARS OF HIGHLIGHTS

May 1985:	Initial public offering
May 1986:	Voice recognition feature available
November 1989:	Secondary public offering
December 1989:	Dallas corporate headquarters acquired
January 1990:	1000th system shipped
July 1990:	Voice channel architecture introduced
January 1991:	Paris subsidiary established
October 1991:	First InterDial system sold
February 1993:	International sales reach $10 million in fiscal year 1993
March 1993:	Company employment surpasses 300 people
May 1993:	3000th system shipped

Opposite: From left to right, Rob-Roy Graham, CFO; Dan Hammond, chairman and CEO; and Mike Barker, president and COO. In 1994 Barker took over for David Brandenburg, who was beginning to step back.

Above: A group of InterVoice employees celebrating the 1994 Dallas Cowboys' Super Bowl appearance. From left are Gary Strzinek, unknown, Jeff Rutherford, and Keith Gyssler. By this time, the conversion to OS/2 was complete.

Right: Kathy Hackney was among the company's first ten employees. She began as office manager and later moved into human resources.

position designed to allow him to gradually step back. He would retire fully within a year. Dan Hammond remained chairman and CEO.

Also that year, Don Brown joined as vice president of human resources. He brought the discipline and experience of a seasoned professional to the human resources department as others had already done in the accounting, legal, manufacturing, and sales departments.

"I remember the culture at that time as very fast paced," Brown said. "It was 'Let's go build something and get it out of the door.' There was very little interest in processes, procedures, anything like that. But to grow, we had to put things like that in place. We spent a fair amount of time educating the managers and explaining to them that if we're going to become a half-billion-dollar or billion-dollar company, these are the kinds of things we have to put in place."[55]

Brown had another immediate concern. Throughout the 1990s, the U.S. technology industry experienced one of business history's longest booms, fueling a decade of economic expansion. As companies expanded, unemployment dropped across the nation. In some places, the unemployment rate actually reached zero—which was considered theoretically impossible. In Dallas, where InterVoice was one of many tech companies along the Telecom Corridor, competition for software engineers was fierce. They could choose among two dozen companies within a two-mile radius, according to Brown.

"When I started, the company experienced very little turnover," Brown said. "The culture and everything here helped to keep people around, and pay was not a big issue. Employees were working here because they loved the product. But as we really started to grow and hire a lot of people, everybody else was too, and there started to be a shortage of people. The company's focus was, one, keeping and retaining good talent, and, two, going out and finding good talent."[56]

This strategy meant keeping the company culture attractive and the benefits plan competitive. To help in this effort, Dan Hammond encouraged his longtime office manager and assistant, Kathy Hackney, to move into the new role of benefits manager.

"I really wasn't trained for it, and I didn't know that I wanted to do it," Hackney said in 2001. "But Dan said, 'You're going to do this. It's the best thing for you.' I can look back now and say he knew more than I did. He had a lot of confidence in me to give me the opportunity, but I did miss the daily interaction with him."[57]

Towards Interactive Information

Throughout its short history, InterVoice's singular focus on voice automation, along with its dedication to 100 percent customer satisfaction, had provided cutting-edge solutions in a continuously expanding and rapidly growing marketplace. The company gained national recognition when *Forbes* magazine named it one of the two hundred best small companies in America in November 1994.

InterVoice was named one of the nation's two hundred best companies by *Forbes* magazine in November 1994. This was the first of several national recognitions it received.

By the mid-1990s, the call-automation industry was poised to move beyond a voice-oriented delivery system. The interactive information response (IIR) solution was evolving, and traditional divisions among technologies were becoming increasingly blurred. Movies on demand, shopping at home, and video phones were becoming fact.[58]

Hammond's vision was that InterVoice would provide complete voice and data network access, fully integrated with customer information and telephone systems, with full communication among all the members of those networks. "This means we are talking to the data side—the mainframes, the databases, the servers, and the voice side—telephone networks and switches, all through peer-to-peer communication," he had said in a 1992 interview.[59]

InterVoice had developed a true multiapplication platform—OneVoice—that enabled it to provide an interactive format for voice, high-resolution graphics, and high-speed data. Even more exciting, OneVoice had positioned InterVoice for the next evolutionary step: the introduction of multimedia capabilities. With simple system upgrades, it would soon be possible for InterVoice customers to enjoy the benefits of the "information superhighway" with audio and enhanced visual elements.

InterVoice began pouring the foundations of that superhighway and designing the interchanges it would need. In the next few years, management would work closely with the Distributed Computer Telephony (DCT) Standards Committee, helping to set the standards that would regulate the industry for years to come.

By the end of 1995, with sales of $76 million and 485 employees, InterVoice was a recognized IVR leader poised on the brink of becoming a $100 million company. Its challenge: to continue its leadership role into a new era of information technology, one in which computers, telephones, fax machines, electronic mail, and even video images would revolutionize the way people communicated.

An InterVoice trade show booth in 1995. By this time, the company had grown to almost $100 million in yearly revenue.

CHAPTER FOUR

AN OPEN VISION

1995–1999

For the first ten years, up until the mid-1990s, there was a lot of cama-
raderie. We used to have Christmas parties, and we had pool parties.
So yeah, those are fond memories.

—Dwain Hammond

BY THE MID-1990S, ANOTHER technological revolution was already in full swing. The first wave of change, launched by the personal computer, swept through American life in the 1980s. In the 1990s, those computers would be tied together by the Internet.

The possibilities offered by this global network of computers were dazzling. New Internet companies were born almost daily, offering every sort of service imaginable, from selling consumer products like pet food to realigning the travel industry. Every area of life was affected by this flood of information and multiplication of communications options, and people rapidly flocked to the Internet. In 1994, three thousand Web sites catered to thirty million users; by 1998, the number of users had jumped fivefold, and the number of Web sites had skyrocketed by more than 6,000 percent.[1]

Not only did daily life change for millions of consumers across America; the economic landscape changed dramatically too. Buoyed by technology companies and the biggest boom in worker productivity since the Industrial Revolution, the stock market rallied, and the U.S. economy began to grow by about four percent annually. Suddenly it became normal for Internet companies to declare public offerings long before they had ever turned a profit. A mere business plan was often

enough to turn an enterprising techie into a multimillionaire.

Interestingly, InterVoice was not part of the Internet boom of the 1990s despite being a proven company with advanced voice technology. Amazingly, only ten years after InterVoice and its cousins founded an industry, speech recognition and IVR were considered old school in the high-flying, sometimes fanciful world of mid-1990s stock valuations. Yet even while the company was challenged to remind the financial markets of its stability and technology, the writing on the wall was clear: One day, after all the data streams converged, the Internet and all the computer networks would reembrace interactive voice systems. And InterVoice would be there.

The competition, of course, would be fierce. By the mid-1990s, open architectures were being developed in almost every IT discipline, and modern networks increasingly included a highly integrated web of platforms, protocols, and devices. Accordingly, companies from AT&T to Periphonics to Hewlett-Packard jumped into the fray.

The Hammond family, including, left to right, Dwain, Carol, Dan, and Mac in the back row and parents William and Volina in the front row, on a 1998 fiftieth anniversary cruise for William and Volina

Faced with multiplying demands from customers for compatibility with a variety of networking technologies and standards, InterVoice realized early on that its success would depend upon developing standard products and technologies.[2] As companies increasingly migrated towards Windows NT and UNIX platforms, InterVoice needed the ability to seamlessly integrate with many different operating systems. To respond, it began two projects, one to bring its hardware in line with developing industry standards and another to create software based on open architecture.[3]

"We had a strong OS/2-based product, and we added UNIX to the mix with VoicePlex," said Abhay Sawant, an engineer who joined InterVoice during the 1994 VoicePlex acquisition. "But OS/2 was in decline and NT was on the horizon. We went through about a year of internal debate as to how to operate in a multi-operating-system environment. Finally, I would say, we came to the right decision."[4]

The decision was to develop a next generation of software that was operating-system independent. This effort was called the Apollo project.

At the same time, InterVoice made another change in its platform. Since about 1991, its hardware platform had been based on microchannel architecture, but by the mid-1990s, with microchannel losing market share, InterVoice realized it would have to replace its hardware platform with a more open technology. That project was named Viper. Unlike Apollo, Viper was a secret. No one in the company outside the hardware engineering department and Dan Hammond himself knew it was operating.

The Business of the Web

The need for open architectures, in both hardware and software, had great implications. As traditional brick-and-mortar companies evaluated strategies and adopted Internet applications, Web services proliferated across the entire communications landscape. Traditional telcos, which had been operating as Internet service providers (ISPs) for some time, found themselves competing with new ISPs to offer voice services. And both generations faced the emergence of application service providers (ASPs), which provided a one-stop shop for Web services, including voice-over-IP (Internet

protocol), data, and rented Web-based applications. The hosting of Web sites and data services by ASPs proved that businesses no longer needed to buy the latest equipment and applications to gain a competitive edge—they could simply "rent" from service providers.[5]

Before long, many businesses began to outsource whole operations to Web-based vendors. One of the most likely candidates for outsourcing was the call center, which was already highly automated. This trend in telecom outsourcing and managed services would continue into the next century as companies sought ways to cut costs and focus on product development, marketing, and customer service.[6] Before long, analysts began predicting an enormous increase in the ASP market. Datamonitor claimed that the global ASP market would reach $5.1 billion by 2001, while Durlacher Research predicted that the European ASP market would grow from $100 million in 2000 to $1.5 billion in just one year.[7]

It was also clear that Internet telephony was poised to compete more and more with traditional telephone service. Long-distance giants such as AT&T, British Telecom, and Deutsche Telekom were experimenting with voice-over-IP, and many predicted that by the beginning of the twenty-first century, one-third to one-half of all voice communications would be carried over the Internet.[8]

Ever Changing Market Requirements

To help its move toward standard, open products, InterVoice continued to invest heavily in research and development—an effort that consumed about 10 percent of total revenue—and to refine its quality assurance and production processes. The effort to formalize manufacturing paid off when InterVoice attained ISO 9001 certification in 1995. ISO 9001 is the most comprehensive of the International Standards Organization (ISO) standards, addressing design, development, installation, production, and service processes.

"We really had to establish standards because if we didn't, we would never have been able to get to ISO 9001, which is all based on higher processes," recalled Marc Gardner.[9] In February 1996, after only one review, InterVoice received another ISO 9001 certification. In August 1997, InterVoice passed its fifth ISO 9001 audit with a perfect score of zero noncompliances.

Products also rolled out with regularity. In July 1995, InterVoice announced the release of MediaConnect, a multimedia connectivity product for IVR. The product enabled users to connect with remote databases and other information sources over standard telephone or ISDN lines. VisualConnect, a World Wide Web connectivity option supported by the OneVoice software agent platform, followed shortly.

Deeper into Telecommunications

Although it still represented only about a quarter of revenue, telecommunications continued to play an important part in the company's revenue picture. Between 1994 and 1995, MCI alone purchased $17 million in InterVoice products for its 1-800-COLLECT system.

At the same time, InterVoice signed several distribution agreements with major companies. A distribution agreement with Sprint led to a $6 million sale to banking giant First Union. The relationship with Siemens, signed in September 1994, continued to move automated call-processing products in the European market. And a joint distributing agreement with DSC Communications would market systems to regional Bell companies and other telecommunications service providers. InterVoice's platform now provided services such as prepaid and postpaid calling card, prepaid wireless, international callback, and one-number service.[10]

By 1995, the InterVoice Telecommunications Systems Division was under the management of Sohail Sattar, the founder and president of VoicePlex. Reporting to Sattar were Steve Polsky, vice president, telco operations; Mark Jones, vice president, sales; and Marc Gardner, vice president, telco engineering.[11]

InterVoice quickly developed a solid reputation as "the name behind the names you know" in telecommunications. The company's customers included names like MCI, Sprint, GTE, and British Telecom. Its telco channel included sales of OneVoice and UNIX-based call-automation platforms to GTE, LDDS, CANTX, U.S. West's wireless operation, and MCI.

By 1996, the telecommunications products market was expected to grow 20 to 25 percent annually, and InterVoice held 9 percent of the market.[12] *Smart Money* magazine predicted that InterVoice would benefit once the pending Telecommunications Act of 1996 took effect.

InterVoice's biggest competitor is AT&T, which controls about 17 percent of the domestic market. But roughly half of that business is to internal AT&T units. And the impending breakup of Ma Bell (again) will make the expansion of external revenue difficult. Why? Because AT&T's success in this business has been buoyed by a marketing strategy of bundling its voice automation technologies with its long-distance packages. After the breakups, these two parts of AT&T are slated to be in different units.[13]

The ISO 9001 banner outside InterVoice's headquarters. Throughout the 1990s, the company adopted standards and practices, earning its ISO certification on its first attempt.

Dwain Hammond, left, with Robert France, research and development, and Lee Huber, staff engineer, at a 1996 employee meeting. That year, InterVoice had to replace revenue lost when its largest customer, MCI, finished its 1-800-COLLECT system.

The Telecommunications Act of 1996

The fact that an industry journalist was writing about a new AT&T breakup in 1996 was a telling indication of how raucous telecommunications had become. In 1984, AT&T had been broken apart by the federal government's trust busters. In 1996, it was torn apart again, this time by market forces.

Only twelve years after the 1984 antitrust settlement, cracks were already beginning to appear. By making the long distance segment of the business competitive but leaving local service in the hands of monopolies—the Baby Bells—the divestiture led to startling contrasts over the next decade.[14] Long distance rates fell, but local rates rose 13 percent as the Bells exploited their local monopolies. By the 1990s, the stage was set for the Telecommunications Act of 1996, which was signed into law by President Bill Clinton on February 8, 1996.

As the first major rewrite of the Communications Act of 1934, it was designed to give the nation a public telecommunications policy for the twenty-first

century. The new law erased all the old boundaries and unleashed competition across the local communications spectrum in the United States, allowing any company to compete in any industry. Consumers could order long distance from their regional Bell, cable TV from their long-distance phone company, and Internet service from their cable company.

As companies struggled to cover as many bases as possible, convergent services became increasingly popular. To meet the growing demand for combined services, consolidations and mergers became common as companies looked to acquire the services they needed to compete in the marketplace. AT&T began investing hundreds of millions of dollars to build a high-speed broadband cable network.

With new companies jumping into the field and old companies struggling for new markets, the U.S. telecommunications equipment industry grew to $91.5 billion in 1999. Industry analyst Dataquest estimated that data traffic in the United States was increasing four times faster than voice traffic.[15]

But just five years after the Act was passed, many were calling for the law to be modified, if not altogether reworked. Although the bill had brought lower telephone rates and wireless competition, it had not brought about true broadband competition. While competitive local exchange carriers (CLECs) accused the Bells of stalling in the local phone market to maintain a regulatory advantage, the Bells accused cable companies of stalling in the broadband market for the same reason. About the only point of agreement among telecom companies, regulators, and legislators was that the landmark act of 1996 hadn't quite worked.[16]

A Sales Trough

In part due to confusion in the telecommunications market after the 1996 deregulation, and also because MCI had finished buying systems for its 1-800-COLLECT, InterVoice's sales

Opposite: In 1995, *Forbes* magazine featured Dan Hammond and InterVoice in a profile. The company had sales of $76 million and was on *Forbes'* list of 200 Best Small Companies. *(Reprinted by permission of* Forbes *magazine, July 3, 1995, issue.)*

Dan Hammond refused to listen when people said mainframes had a better future than PCs, which is why InterVoice is such a successful company today.

Young man in a hurry

By Toddi Gutner Block

IF YOU WANT to move money from your bank savings account to your checking account, you might choose to do it by phone. A technology known as IVR (for interactive voice response) uses recorded voice to lead you through the process, telling you what your balances are and how to transfer your money using your voice, a telephone keypad or a personal computer keyboard.

The $800 million market for IVR systems is highly fragmented, with some 150 players in North America. But one stands head and shoulders above the crowd: Dallas-based Inter-Voice, Inc., a repeat member on FORBES' 200 Best Small Companies in America annual listings. Last year InterVoice ranked 157th on the list, with earnings of $13 million (80 cents a share) on sales of $76 million. Revenues this year are likely to hit $94 million, according to Herbert Tinger, First Albany analyst. That gives InterVoice about 9% of the IVR market. With its stock recently trading at 15⅛ a share, InterVoice's market cap currently exceeds $230 million.

InterVoice's chief executive and cofounder is an energetic young electrical engineer named Daniel Ham-

Photographs by Doug Milner

Daniel Hammond, cofounder and chief executive officer of InterVoice

"I'm never satisfied unless I'm living a little bit on the edge."

flattened between 1996 and 1998 at $97 million, $102 million, and $104 million respectively. Although Wall Street didn't like flat sales, Hammond considered it an achievement to maintain sales after MCI, the company's biggest customer, had stopped buying systems and while many telecommunications companies were delaying the purchase of call automation systems until the market settled down.[17]

"Our stock plummeted as we flattened out," said Hammond. "But the fact of the matter is that we did pretty well considering we got zero out of our biggest customer."[18]

While InterVoice was working to build sales, it was also going through an internal transition. InterVoice Vice Chairman David Brandenburg, who had by this time exceeded his original three-year employment contract, returned to retirement in June 1995 and pursued personal philanthropy. Brandenburg wouldn't remain away for long, however—he returned to the board of directors within two years.

Around the same time Brandenburg was coming back to the board, Mike Barker, president and COO, left InterVoice to pursue a position with another technology company. He was replaced as president by David Berger, a computer industry veteran with seventeen years of experience at IBM.

CEO Dan Hammond remained deeply involved with the daily operations of the company, and the rest of the executive team stayed intact. Costume parties were still the norm during the holidays, and the existing management team, many of whom were now five- or six-year veterans, continued to make their presence felt. A popular story circulates about the 1997 combined employee and shareholders meeting, when the InterVoice All Star Band, headlined by CFO Rob-Roy Graham, gave a surprise performance of the Steppenwolf classic "Born to be Wild."

"Employees love to see senior management step out of the traditional and perceived roles," said Graham.

The year before that meeting, we ended up at the karaoke bar of the hotel, and Dan Hammond likes karaoke. He persuaded me to sing "Born to be Wild," and the story began to propagate amongst the employee base, and people began to wonder if

The employee party in 1996 at the Hotel InterContinental in Addison. Beginning that year, InterVoice headed into a period of flat sales, partially because of deregulation and partly because of the lost MCI business.

it was really true. So the following year, in 1997, at the shareholders' meeting, we decided to capitalize on the rumor and demonstrate that I'd actually done that.[19]

Viper and Apollo

The race for new technology was intense. InterVoice pursued markets across the entire business spectrum, chasing down customers in everything from prepaid calling cards to transcript services for school districts. To better serve these multiple markets, in May 1997 InterVoice announced a reorganization that split the company vertically into four groups to develop and sell call-automation products and service to companies in the call center, financial, employee benefit, and health care industries.

InterVoice was also planning to bring out its next-generation products. Both the company's operating system and its hardware platform used IBM's OS/2 operating system and microchannel hardware, which weren't making permanent inroads into the marketplace. By 1997, InterVoice was ready to offer the fruits of the Viper and Apollo projects.

The Viper project was first. In January, InterVoice introduced voice and signal processing boards that were industry standard architecture (ISA) bus compatible. This family of products replaced the generation that had relied on IBM's microchannel architecture. "The microchannel was a fairly stable product that we used for five years," remembered Philip Walden, vice president of manufacturing.

But about the end of that five years, we got wind that IBM was going to abandon the microchannel. So we started a stealth project. It was truly a stealth project, where you actually had to sign a secret document not to tell anybody. What we were developing was a new VocalCard based on the ISA.[20]

This project, Viper, was so secret, recalled Hammond, that employees agreed they could be released from the company if they mentioned it. "We didn't want to slow down current sales," he remembered. "So we had it in a lab downstairs

with a lock on it. I went down there one time, and I walked into the lab, and we had a new technician, who said, 'I'm sorry, sir. You can't come in here.' He threw me out of the lab. But we were successful. No salesman ever found out about it until we had it in production."[21]

Shortly afterward, InterVoice announced the result of the Apollo project: a new version of InterSoft that was compatible with a variety of operating systems, including SCO UNIXware, HP-UX, Windows NT, and OS/2. This new InterSoft was important because InterVoice would no longer be tied to a single operating system. For its launch, InterVoice "had an all-hands meeting where we invited [Apollo astronaut] Alan Bean" to talk to the company, remembered Dan Hammond.[22]

"We wanted to build a product that was transparent to whatever operating system was underneath," Hammond explained. "We also made it transparent to the application development environment so that we were developing only one element of the operating software, not everything."[23]

Clockwise from top left: At the launch of InterVoice's Apollo project, Dan Hammond stands next to Apollo astronaut Alan Bean. Next, Bean poses with InterVoice President Mike Barker. At left, the research and development team responsible for InterVoice's conversion to open systems and architecture gathers around Bean at the event in 1997.

Even into the mid-1990s,
InterVoice continued to rely
mainly on selling large-enterprise
systems to banks and other institutions.
Telecommunications sales were rising but still
represented less than 30 percent of overall sales.

This time around, InterVoice was much more careful as it migrated its product platform; the OS/2 lessons had been learned very well. The company handled the project in three phases (also named for elements of the space program) and was careful not to build up customer expectations before its release.

In 1997, InterVoice's Mondex Gateway was chosen to handle the remote transfer of electronic funds in the Smartcard program launched by Chase Manhattan Bank and MasterCard International. The Gateway, running on InterVoice's OneVoice platform, enabled merchants to deposit funds daily from their point-of-sale devices, making it possible for participating banks, consumers, and merchants to transfer electronic currency among each other.[24]

In February 1998, InterVoice purchased the Enhanced Services Platform (ESP) product line from Integrated Telephony Products for $5.2 million. The acquisition allowed InterVoice to begin marketing an Internet-based solution to long-distance, wireless, and local carriers that used Internet telephony. The decision quickly proved fruitful: Orders totaling $5 million for the new ESP solutions rolled in within ninety days.[25]

In June 1998, InterVoice announced the availability of RealCareRemote, a service that remotely monitored and tested InterVoice systems twenty-four hours a day, seven days a week.

Traditional Markets Stay Strong

The telecommunications market in particular remained a company strength, and InterVoice never strayed from its formula for success: customized configurations tailored to meet each customer's requirements.

InterVoice partnered with leaders such as Hewlett-Packard (H-P), NewNet, and NEC to develop products that were compatible with various architectures. Thanks to the Telecommunications Act, InterVoice was able to provide a number of end-user applications using H-P platforms, including calling card, debit card, voice-activated dialing, voice-navigated voice mail, and single-number services.[26]

On the customer premise equipment (CPE) side of the market, InterVoice offered specialized configurations to provide call-processing solutions

for companies such as GeoTel Communications, WilTel, Sungard, U.S. Order, Davox, and others.

In May 1998, InterVoice introduced Agent Connect at CTI World '98 in Toronto, Canada. As a "call center in a box," it was the first turnkey call-center solution that integrated inbound and outbound applications on a single multiapplication platform. Later that year, the first European sale of Agent Connect was shipped to a pan-European broadband service provider.

In September 1998, InterVoice purchased DC Systems' CTI and call-center software suite for $4.5 million. In addition to giving InterVoice indirect worldwide distribution capabilities, the acquisition opened up opportunities in the broader CTI market segment.[27]

The Market Roars Back

The company's optimism in its products and markets was justified. By 1999, sales had grown better than 25 percent to upwards of $130 million. Some of this increase was driven by yet another new source of business: Year 2000 (Y2K) compliance. Although the public and mainstream media later perceived it to have been a false alarm, the "millennium bug" presented a real danger to the world's computer networks: They were predicted to revert on January 1 to 1900.

"I headed up the operation to get organized for Y2K," recalled company Vice President Gordon Givens.

We spent probably eighteen months getting ready. We had upgrade programs. We had a system we could use to actually analyze all the applications we had deployed. We even got to the point that I had my group develop a little map of the world, and we tracked the hour as it went around the world. We tracked the number of problems so we could prewarn people about issues. We even had some of our bigger accounts in the United States on the phone because they wanted to know if we had a program in place.[28]

At the same time, revenue was also helped by a general conversion to Windows NT, which required that InterVoice upgrade systems.

At left, Hammond stands on top of an old sedan at the company Quarterly Bash. Below, employees gather after the event. The car bashing was significant as it symbolized InterVoice's smashing the old systems and converting to new architecture.

"We caught the next wave of people converting to Y2K compliance and putting in NT, getting the new hardware and software, and we had a great run," recalled Dan Hammond.[29]

Selling Systems Worldwide

When Gordon Givens began working on the Y2K problem, he had just returned from Europe, where he had once again set up an InterVoice office. In 1996, the company moved its European headquarters from Paris to London, even relocating many of the France-based employees. From London, Givens had overseen a global network of dozens of foreign distributors, the largest of which was Siemens.

In February 1997, Siemens signed an agreement with a large Asian telco provider to deliver $4.6 million in InterVoice network services platform (NSP) 5000 systems. Seimens accounted for more than 10 percent of the company's total sales during fiscal 1997.

In 1998, InterVoice opened an office in Brazil, increasing its presence in the rapidly developing Latin American market. During the year the company would experience significant activity in Venezuela due to the growing popularity of enhanced services for wireless providers.[30]

As InterVoice expanded its worldwide operations, it continued to add senior managers to its team. In September 1998, it announced the addition of M. Gregory Smith as senior vice president of sales

for the Americas and Asia Pacific. Smith brought more than sixteen years of telecommunications experience to the company, including eleven years with Rolm/IBM/Siemens. The addition of Smith allowed InterVoice to enhance its marketing organization by promoting Dick Herrman, who had been responsible for sales and marketing, to the position of senior vice president, corporate marketing.

Speech Technology Heats Up

By the late 1990s, IVR technology had become accepted in certain markets, including telecommunications, finance, banking, and insurance. It was, in fact, such an accepted part of normal business life that the products had become commodified a bit. "It became more a production-type operation," remembered Givens. "Everybody was putting in somewhat the same system."[31] InterVoice, with its ISO 9001 designation and open systems, fared pretty well in this environment.

The future, however, lay with another burgeoning technology. Speech recognition technology had spent decades in the laboratory, but by 1999 PC speech programs claimed 95 percent accuracy and

could recognize continuous speech, thus eliminating the need to pause between words—a major drawback of earlier systems. Intel noted that speech

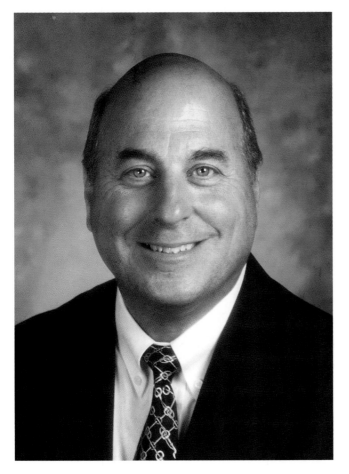

technology "is ready to become a critical element of the PC user interface—and for good reason."[32]

InterVoice was prepared. Through its own development and a partnership with Speechworks, InterVoice had some of the world's finest speech-recognition technology. Walt Mirkowicz, a development engineer and later vice president of the platform product unit for the network division, remarked that a traditional InterVoice strength was its ability to stay just ahead of the technological curve. "We make sure we keep our products at the proper level," Mirkowicz said, "and I believe that we've always been perceived as a driving force in the industry."[33]

Contenders in the fast-growing market included Lernout & Hauspie; Dragon Systems, a U.S. pioneer; and mainstream vendors such as Philips and IBM, which alone had more than two hundred people dedicated to the research, product development, and marketing of speech technology.[34]

Above: Employees gather at the 1997 Quarterly Bash in the company garage. The crowd was celebrating InterVoice's recent conversion from the old software system to a new, open system.

Left: David Berger was named company president in 1998. He had an extensive background in telecommunications and computers.

As a result of increased computing power and demand, the market for speech-enabled applications was believed to have extraordinary potential. Voice Information Associates, a U.S. market research company, estimated that the market for advanced speech technology would mushroom from $460 million in 1997 to $5 billion in 2001 and $7.9 billion in 2003. Meanwhile, translation services, another rapidly growing segment of the language products market, was projected to grow from $3 billion in 1997 to $5.2 billion in 2001 and $6.9 billion in 2003.[35]

In July 1996, InterVoice—already the first to offer voice recognition—announced an original equipment manufacturing agreement with Applied Languages Technologies (ALTech) to integrate ALTech's large vocabulary voice recognition software into InterVoice's OneVoice software agent platform. As part of the agreement, InterVoice received warrants for ALTech stock. Later, after ALTech had changed its name to Speechworks, those warrants would yield a great return for InterVoice.

The relationship resulted in an industry first: a voice-enabled stock trading service.[36] In December 1997, InterVoice and ALTech announced the use of combined technologies to develop and deploy E*TRADE Group's speech-enabled TELE*MASTER investing system. The landmark event marked the finance industry's first fully speech-enabled, natural-language investing system.

"It was our first big voice-recognition system," remembered engineer Bogdan Blaszczak. "It was a really big development effort."[37]

A project with this scope included a wide range of challenges, but all of them were already familiar, at least in theory, to speech recognition experts. In voice-automated stock recognition, for instance, InterVoice engineers had to build a huge database of vocabulary to include every stock symbol as well as every permutation of company names.

"The system basically had to recognize IBM, Big Blue, every possible name for International Business Machines," said engineer Skip Cave. "There were thousands and thousands of names for stocks, and it had to recognize them all."[38]

In 1998, InterVoice formed an Advanced Speech Development team to keep the company at the forefront of the emerging speech-recognition market. By 1999, when the market for speech recognition began mushrooming, InterVoice was ready. The company demonstrated SpeechAccess, its family of advanced, integrated, speech recognition products, at CALLcenterLive in February 1999. That spring, InterVoice announced orders for speech-enhanced systems for a major U.S.-based airline and a national transportation company.

In April 1999, InterVoice entered into an OEM agreement with Nuance Communications, a supplier of natural-language speech recognition and speaker verification technologies, to expand its speech-enabled application offerings.

While still evolving, speech technology had finally become viable, offering an exciting way for developers to add value to their software and expand into new arenas. "Originally, we had about twenty words," Cave said, "so we had to figure out how to do everything in twenty words. That was okay, but it was difficult. But in about 1998, computers got fast enough and cheap enough that we were able to expand. We were able to expand single-word vocabularies into thousands of words."[39]

The great benefit of this development was its flexibility. Modern speech recognition technology is known as "directed dialogue." In other words, the computer asks a question and then prompts the customer to give certain answers, such as "last five checks" or "yes" or "no." By asking enough questions, the computer narrows down the customer request and can provide the right information. With the expected increase in power, however, speech recognition programmers envisioned a day when a computer could understand regular human speech spoken in normal sentences. This kind of program, often called artificial intelligence, could be used in customer-help situations, in hand-free mobile telephones, and in many other applications.

In 1999, artificial intelligence remained a gleam in an engineer's eye. "Right now it's fun," said software engineer Myra Hambleton, "but the latest stuff, the stuff that's in the universities, is dealing with what they call natural-language-understand-

Opposite: Advanced speech recognition allowed InterVoice to develop stock quote systems. InterVoice also developed a system for Fidelity that allowed employees access to 401(k) accounts.

ing engines. It's very, very interesting. Think of the tools that we could create to help you deploy applications that understand anything you would say."[40]

As the century came to a close, many analysts foresaw yet another sea change in the telecommunications arena. One 2000 report entitled "Opportunities for Telecom Hosting" predicted that "the battleground" of the future would be "services such as remote access; managed intranet/extranet; e-commerce; voice-over-IP (VoIP); multimedia services; streamed audio/video services; and unified messaging."[41] InterVoice offered many of these.

InterVoice Firsts

THROUGHOUT ITS SHORT HISTORY, InterVoice has earned a record of engineering excellence. The company was the first to bring all applications—from IVR and credit card processing to Internet transaction support—onto a single platform. By 1997, InterVoice had clearly taken a leadership position in technology and call automation, compiling an impressive list of industry firsts.

- First open architecture system
- First to use integrated voice recognition
- First with ISDN and T1/E1 interfaces
- First with an all-digital platform
- First to offer multinode configurations
- First to support the Bellcore Analog Display Services Interface (ADSI)
- First to offer interactive multimedia PC connectivity
- The first multiplatform, Graphical User Interface–based application development and service creation tool
- First Smart Card–IVR integration
- First fully integrated natural-language–large-vocabulary speech recognition
- First platform offering fully integrated call center capabilities[1]

Industry Recognition

As it grew, InterVoice continued to attract the attention of national media. In November 1994, InterVoice had been selected as one of the two hundred best small companies in America by *Forbes* magazine. The next year, it moved even higher in the rankings: *Forbes* named InterVoice one of America's one hundred best small companies.

In a related article entitled "The Honor Roll," InterVoice was included in a listing of only fourteen companies that qualified for inclusion in the listing for five or more years.[42] In addition to earning high scores as a quality company to work for, InterVoice continued to earn industry honors for its groundbreaking products. In its February 1996 issue, *Call Center* magazine named InterVoice's InterDial predictive dialer a 1995 product of the year.

Four leading high-tech market-research firms, Dataquest, Cahners, In-Stat Group, and Frost & Sullivan, named InterVoice the top IVR supplier to the U.S. market in 1997. The next year, Cahners gave top honors to InterVoice for the second consecutive year.[43]

A Worldwide Leader

By the end of 1998, InterVoice had a truly global presence, with 721 employees, offices throughout the world, and nearly twelve thousand systems installed in fifty-two countries. It sold its products directly to end users and more than 130 domestic and international distributors.

From a revenue point of view, sales had also recovered from their mid-1990s slump, once again surging forward by double digits. InterVoice's executive team included Dan Hammond, chairman of the board and chief executive officer; David Berger, president and chief operating officer; Rob-Roy

At right, Dwain and Dan Hammond are third and fourth from the left, respectively, at a company function. Below, Holly and Dan Hammond pose during the 1997 President's Club trip. That year, InterVoice introduced the world's first IVR stock quote system.

yet. The mid-1990s sales slump had a lesson buried in it: building a big, customized telecommunications business might boost revenue, but it wasn't particularly profitable. It wasn't until the Y2K and Windows NT business kicked in that InterVoice once again recorded large earnings. Moreover, InterVoice still derived only about 30 percent of its revenue from the telecommunications market.

For all of these reasons, InterVoice set its sights on an acquisition. The company had acquired technologies and companies before, such as VoicePlex, but they had each been much smaller than Inter-Voice. This time, InterVoice would set its sights on an industry equal, an established technology leader of almost exactly the same size, and one that was almost perfectly matched. That company was Brite Voice Systems, an voice processing company with revenue of about $120 million, offices in Orlando, Florida, and Wichita, Kansas, a huge overseas business, and a leading position in the telecommunications market.

Graham, secretary, chief financial officer, chief accounting officer, and controller; Gordon Givens, senior vice president, custom products; Dwain Hammond, senior vice president, engineering; M. Gregory Smith, senior vice president, sales and marketing; H. Don Brown, vice president, human resources; Dean Howell, vice president and corporate counsel; Victor James, vice president, network services; Michael Polcyn, vice president, packaged products; Eric Pratt, vice president, telco sales; and Philip Walden, vice president, manufacturing.[44]

In 1999, this team of executives, besides dealing with the regular pressures of running and growing a high-tech company, was laying the groundwork for InterVoice's greatest challenge

PART II

FOUNDED IN 1984 BY STAN BRANNAN, Brite Voice Systems had its first success with audiotex services for yellow pages and newspaper publishers. This service allowed callers to access information such as sports, classifieds, and even personal ads.

By the early 1990s, however, Brite's market in audiotex systems was under pressure. The culprit was rapidly advancing technology: Voice mail vendors and others could easily offer similar services for a fraction of the price. In response, Brite Voice began a dramatic transformation. Instead of data portals, Brite pursued cellular voice processing, concentrating on overseas business. At the same time, the company launched a managed-services operation, thinking that teleco providers would rather outsource the function than buy and maintain complicated equipment.

The strategy was a resounding success. As audiotex services dropped into the background, Brite transformed itself into one of the leading global suppliers of IVR telco systems and managed services. In 1996, when Brite signed a massive contract with BT/Cellnet for cellular services in the United Kingdom, the evolution was complete.

But between 1996 and 1998, Brite underwent radical changes in leadership and location. Brannan, the founder and emotional center of the company, stepped down, and the company moved its headquarters to Orlando, Florida. By 1998, after two tumultuous years, Brite Voice Systems was ready for another change. Brannan returned to the company, and conversations soon began with another leading IVR company, InterVoice. Once begun, the process was fast: InterVoice-Brite was born.

The signing ceremony for the Brite Voice Systems contract with BT/Cellnet. From left, front row, are David Booth of BT/Cellnet and Stan Brannan. From left, back row, are Scotty Walsh, John Burnet, and Derrick Edge.

Stan Brannan, founder of Brite Voice Systems in Wichita, Kansas

CHAPTER FIVE

BRITE VOICE: THE EARLY YEARS

1974–1991

*When Stan Brannan gets an idea, he goes after it. It doesn't just sit
on a metal shelf somewhere.*

— John Morrison,
former Brite Voice vice president,
research and development

THE MERGER OF INTERVOICE AND Brite Voice was a long time coming. The companies had first discussed it in the 1980s, tracking each other's progress down slightly different paths in the same industry. In many ways, the similarities between InterVoice and Brite Voice were astonishing. The companies were founded in the same year by engineers who were dedicated to using the microprocessor to enable voice communication. Both had grown quickly, and they were almost the same size.

Yet it was their differences that drew them together. Brite Voice had originally made its fortune in the audiotex portion of the market, selling information databases to a variety of industries. Then it had built a significant managed services business with an established overseas network. These strengths played directly into InterVoice's forte in domestic enterprise systems, or the business of selling complete systems to banks and other institutions.

Brite Voice was the product of one man's ambition: Stan Brannan. Ultimately, Brannan founded several companies with varying degrees of success, but none were as large as Brite Voice. A native of Great Band, Kansas, Brannan founded his first company after two years as an electrical engineer with Boeing Military Aircraft in Wichita, Kansas.[1]

While working at Boeing, the Wichita State University grad, along with friends Larry Runyan and Dean Mehler, began to believe that a revolution was imminent due to the introduction of the microprocessor. In 1974, twenty-four-year-old Brannan used $1,400 of his savings to found Mycro-Tek, a manufacturer of microprocessor-based products used in electronic newsroom systems and television character generators. Six years later, Brannan sold his interest in Mycro-Tek to the company known as AlliedSignal, in Morristown, New Jersey, for $10.3 million. He stayed at Mycro-Tek and eventually became president of one of Allied-Signal's subsidiaries, Mergenthaler Linotype, a Long Island manufacturer of typesetting equipment and laser printers.

But it wouldn't be long before Brannan struck off on his own again. In 1983 he founded Brite Digital Systems with John Morrison, a software developer from Mycro-Tek. Brite Digital was to develop products that enabled the public to use Touch-Tone telephone and cable television channels to access computer-stored information.

Brite Voice was chartered to sell audiotex systems to Yellow Pages, city governments, and other institutions. After a slow start in the mid-1980s, Brite grew rapidly.

However, with only one customer—Telecommunication of Denver—the company went bankrupt by October 1984. Despite the business failure, important groundwork had been laid, for it was at Brite Digital that Brannan developed StockQuote Hotline, the foundation for the future Brite Voice.

In late 1984, Brannan tried yet again, founding Brite Voice Systems at 555 North Woodlawn in Wichita, Kansas. In its early days the company employed six people and had just two products: StockQuote Hotline, which enabled people to access stock quotes over the phone, and CITYLINE, an audiotex service Brannan designed that was used by media companies. Both products allowed the public to access computer-stored information via a Touch-Tone telephone—a revolutionary concept in the early 1980s.

"The technology that was coming out then allowed a personal computer to answer a telephone and speak in a computerized voice, offering the ability to provide real cost savings," remembered Brannan. "That technology was so new that very few companies were doing it."[2]

This put Brite Voice in a slightly different segment of the market from InterVoice, which was

The Brite office on Woodlawn in Wichita, Kansas, in 1989. Stan Brannan, CEO and chairman of the board, is third from the left.

pushing the IVR market forward while Brite concentrated on audiotex sales to media outlets. Brannan was convinced that Brite could differentiate itself by providing a turnkey system.[3]

Hanging Tough

In the beginning, Brite appeared destined for failure. Its systems, which comprised specially configured computer equipment and proprietary software that provided a reliable, cost-effective alternative to live telephone operators, seemed radical, and many customers and businesses resisted the idea of using automation to replace a live operator.

But Brannan wouldn't give up easily. Having already created two companies and rebounded from a failed start-up, he was determined to succeed, and before long an opportunity presented itself. A customer requested a product to fill a particular need, and the Brite Voice Gateway 5000 was born. The Gateway 5000 was an audiotex system for service bureaus handling large volumes of calls requesting information or placing orders for products.[4]

The Gateway system used large computers that served thousands of different information providers and customers. The telephone number dialed told the computer which application the caller was trying to access. One advantage of this approach was that hundreds or even thousands of information providers shared investment in hardware and lines. Placing an information system on a very large system also gave each information provider access to multiple lines for peak calling loads generated by television or radio advertising bursts.[5]

In 1985, when the U.K. market launched its counterpart to the American pay-per-call 900-number telephone service, Brite began providing Gateway systems to companies in England. At the time, Brite was one of the leading vendors offering systems in the five-hundred- to five-thousand-port range with interactive capability.[6]

Despite the innovative nature of its products, Brite struggled to find its market, reporting losses of $132,000 in 1984, $205,000 in 1985, and $64,000 in 1986. "The company was in a true start-up phase where 90 percent of the companies

Left: The Brite office in Canton, Massachusetts. Headquartered in Wichita, Brite quickly expanded its geographical reach throughout North America and into Europe.

Below: The engineering department in Canton, Massachusetts. Scott Brannan, Stan's brother, is on the left. Throughout the 1980s, the company steadily expanded into new markets with new technologies.

like it usually go broke in the first eighteen months to two years—and we darn near did that," recalled David Martin, former Brite Voice vice president of sales. "But Stan Brannan's personal belief was extended to all of us, and it pulled us through. We learned that you have to believe."[7]

Slowly, the firm began to grow as it identified emerging markets in health care, real estate, and cellular telephones.

"The company started with a few relatively small ideas to offer telephone response equipment to newspapers and television stations to allow them to give readers or viewers up-to-date information," Brannan said. "The company expanded as the opportunities presented themselves in other market areas, including interactive lines for classified advertising, real estate lines, bank information lines, and a variety of public service lines."[8]

Out of the CITYLINE concept evolved voice directory systems, or the "talking yellow pages," which was sold to yellow-pages publishers and telephone companies. In addition, Telecare was developed for hospitals and first established at HCA Wesley Hospital in Wichita, Kansas, in October 1987. The system provided interactive voice information for patients, employees, and doctors.[9]

Real Estate Hotline, introduced in October 1988, allowed home buyers to peruse real estate listings according to geographic area, price range, and home features. Potential home buyers accessed Hotline through a Touch-Tone telephone.[10]

Many have attributed Brite's longevity during the difficult start-up years to Stan Brannan's personal vision. John Morrison, Brannan's long-time friend and Brite Digital cofounder, later became vice president of research and development at Brite Voice. He remembered what it was like to work for the innovative and driven entrepreneur.

This is a man who has got the brains, the drive, and yet the compassion to deal with people in a high-tech environment. We work our fannies off around here, but Stan Brannan outworks any of us. The pace of the pack is set by the pace of the leader. I think Stan has built a team of people who are in his image and likeness—and I think that's why the company is where it is today.[11]

For his part, Brannan always insisted that his company was successful because of its talented and dedicated employees. "We really pulled together during those high-growth years when it was a small start-up," he said. "The employees we were able to assemble during those years and the hard work and the dedication they showed were really remarkable."[12]

Brite's culture fit the classic entrepreneurial model—people learned by the seat of their pants, wore many hats, and figured things out on the fly.

"They started the company with engineers who got together and built the products. Everybody was a salesman and everybody was an engineer, and there wasn't any real structure to it," recalled Scott Walsh, a Brite executive vice president. "When you wanted to make a decision, you just went ahead and did it. You didn't have to ask anybody."[13]

Funding Its Growth

Throughout the 1980s, when investors were steering clear of young, high-tech companies, Brite sorely needed venture capital. It had always maintained a conservative cash position rather than borrow heavily to keep up with its growth—but by the late 1980s, it needed outside funding for future growth.

Finding it difficult to convince Kansas investors to invest in his high-tech business, Brannan solicited investors in St. Louis, Denver, and Texas before finding Commercial Federal Corporation of Nebraska, the holding company that owned Commercial Federal Savings and Loan Association. In late 1987, Commercial Federal, located in Omaha, took a 25 percent equity interest in Brite, providing $2.8 million for the company's growth.[14]

That year Brite showed its first profit. Sales in 1987 were $3 million, followed by 1988 sales of $6.1 million—more than six times the revenue reported in 1985.[15] Its workforce, which began with six employees in 1987, ended the year at twenty-six.

It's safe to say that 1987 was the beginning of the future for Brite Voice. Its period as an unknown upstart with strange products was over. A powerful new medium, voice services, offered the opportunity to disseminate information and communicate effectively while cutting labor costs and saving time. Voice services also cost little, stayed open twenty-four hours a day, and provided capabilities for follow-up and other information management.[16]

Over the previous three years, Brite had developed a reputation as a leader in the audiotex industry. Telecommunication service providers accounted for the majority of Brite sales: call automation systems and services that incorporated prepaid/postpaid applications, voice response, voice recognition, voice/facsimile messaging, audiotex, and interactive customer applications in both standard products and customized market solutions.

Audiotex systems had been purchased by more than thirty clients nationwide under the CITYLINE trademark and by forty worldwide. Brite also offered the only equipment commercially available to capture information from the Associated Press Stockquote Wire and DowPhone.

Moving Overseas

Another major reason for Brite's 1987 jump in revenue, beside product acceptance, had to do with a fortuitous distribution agreement. That year, the company signed with Marconi Company Limited in the United Kingdom for a five-year exclusive distributorship in Great Britain, Northern Ireland, and Australia. Within a year, Marconi accounted for about 16 percent of Brite's revenue.[17]

In December 1988, branching out even further, Brite developed a turnkey information service that allowed cellular telephone service providers to offer their customers information relevant in their daily lives. CIN, Brite's Cellular Information Network, allowed cell phone customers to access information in more than nine hundred categories, including StockQuote Hotline, business, sports, entertainment, self-improvement, and road services.

The IPO

Even with rapidly increasing sales—or perhaps because of them—Brite still needed additional funding, so in 1989, Brannan, the majority shareholder, elected to take his company public. That year, Brite became the first Wichita company to initiate a successful IPO since American Restaurant Partners in 1987. It didn't hurt, of course, that sales had been doubling and

Glenn Etherington, chief financial officer of Brite Voice. Comprising Brannan, Etherington, and Scott Walsh, Brite's management structure was very flat and fast.

tripling each year. For the six-month period ending June 30, 1989, Brite Voice reported revenues of $8.67 million—a 194 percent increase over the $2.95 million reported in the same period in 1988.[18]

The successful offering called for the sale of 1.5 million shares, which opened at $12.50 each and raised $11.6 million for the company and $5.8 million for key stockholders and the underwriters.[19] Traded on the NASDAQ exchange under the symbol BVSI, the stock immediately earned a spot on the *Wall Street Journal*'s most-active list, 87,200 shares traded. The issue closed the first day trading at $14.[20]

Before the offering could happen, however, Brite's prospectus required a last-minute revision because of a contract dispute with a major customer, 900 Services. The Omaha-based company was dissatisfied with a Gateway system it had purchased in February 1989 for $1.72 million, and it refused to pay a balance due of $614,000. Brite filed a countersuit in September in U.S. District Court in Kansas for the balance of the account. The suit would eventually be settled out of court, with Brite taking a small write-down.

Despite the pending litigation, the IPO was completed on September 6, 1989. "It was interesting," remembered Glenn Etherington, Brite CFO. "We took the company public on an upswing, but we had an interesting experience trying to get the public offering with that information swirling around the stock."[21]

Ron Smith, vice president and branch manager at the Wichita office of B. C. Christopher Securities, said investor interest in the offering was strong and noted the lawsuit had little effect on the subsequent trading.[22]

"For a small offer of 1.5 million shares, the offering was substantially oversubscribed," Smith said. "This offering was in demand all around the country, and quite frankly there was greater demand out of the Wichita area. Many successful public companies have come out of Wichita. But this offering of Brite Voice Systems has the potential to be one of the next great Wichita companies."[23]

For Brannan, who had reduced his holding from 51 percent to 33 percent in conjunction with the offering, the IPO meant he could give something back to the loyal employees who formed the backbone of Brite.

"It was the first public company that I had been CEO of, and it was an opportunity for me to take employees I thought were working very hard to grow the business and let them share in the wealth of the company they were creating," Brannan said. "It was an excellent experience for me because it gave me the tools to help my employees participate in the growth of the company."[24]

At the time of the IPO, the company's three major products were CITYLINE, Voice Directory, and Gateway 5000. Markets for its products were widespread, with CITYLINE systems in use by companies such as Knight-Ridder, Times Mirror, and KWCH-TV in Wichita. In November 1989, Brite announced the sale of its thirty-fourth CITYLINE audiotex system to the Chronicle Publishing Company's newspaper division in San Francisco. The Bay area became the newspaper division's third CITYLINE network, joining the *Pantagraph* and the *Worcester Telegram and Gazette.*

Other major media companies using Brite's equipment included Cox, Hearst, *London Financial Times*, ABC/Capital Cities, Ottoway Newspapers, and Hubbard Broadcasting.[25] Brite's Voice Directory had been installed in ninety markets, and its Gateway 5000 customers included Sprint Services, a division of United Telecommunications, and 900 Services.[26]

Following the completion of its successful IPO, Brite was positioned for rapid growth. The company planned to use its share of the proceeds from the IPO for a wide variety of purposes, including working capital, product development, acquisitions, and expansion or possible relocation of the company.[27]

Construction of the new headquarters in Wichita. Although Brannan had considered moving Brite to a larger city with greater access to capital, he ultimately elected to keep it in Wichita, building the new headquarters in 1990. The finished building is in the background.

The Decade Ends

By the end of the 1980s, one thing was clear to the telecom industry: The battle for market share across the economy would be won by companies that were willing to utilize new technology and techniques to reach their target audience.

St. Paul Medical Center in Dallas joined that group when it introduced Telecare in November 1989 by inserting a directory in the Sunday edition of the *Dallas Morning News*. One of Brite's newest products, Telecare provided health care facilities with a unique marketing opportunity to provide health care information twenty-four hours a day. Topics ranging from alcoholism to cancer to heart disease were available to residents who lived within the calling area.[28]

Even when Brite's stock tumbled in late 1989, many analysts continued to support the company, believing that its fundamentals were solid and its prospect for growth was strong. The stock closed at $10 in November 1989, down from a $14.25 high.

Two analysts who followed the company—Scott Stephenson, of B. C. Christopher in Kansas City, Missouri, and Tom Friedberg, of Piper, Jaffray & Hopwood in Seattle—admitted they were mystified by the drop, especially in light of the company's positive third-quarter earnings report. For the third quarter, ended September 30, 1989, Brite reported income of $866,000 on revenues of $3.36 million, which compared well with income of

The completed building at 739 East Twenty-first Street in Wichita. The new space measured forty thousand square feet and accommodated the growing staff.

$322,000 on revenues of $1.67 million for the comparable quarter the previous year.[29]

The only reason Stephenson and Friedberg could advance for the drop was that the whole industry had been weakened. "We know of no fundamental reason for the drop," Stephenson said. "In the industry itself, the stock prices have been weak. The only thing we can think of is that it was a high P/E (price/earnings) stock to begin with and there's relatively small emerging growth in the market."[30]

Although the lawsuit with 900 Services was still pending, both Stephenson and Friedberg said they didn't believe the litigation was having an effect on Brite's trading volume or its stock price, and plenty of reasons remained to be bullish on Brite stock. In late 1989, the company announced that Marconi, its British partner, had placed an order for twenty audiotex systems.

"Marconi has been an excellent distributor for Brite over the years," Brannan later commented. "They have placed close to one hundred systems in the United Kingdom since our initial agreement in 1986. They were one of our first, and continue to be one of our largest customers."[31]

As it entered the last decade of the century, Brite was on a roll. Revenues in 1989 exploded from $6.1 million the previous year to $15.6 million—mostly fueled by large orders for its new product line, the Gateway 5000. The systems, which were marketed to toll-free 800-number and pay-per-call 900-number service bureaus, sold for between $20,000 and $1,000,000 and were used by major customers such as Sprint Gateways and 900 Services.

A New Era

Obviously, Brite was heading into the 1990s in a good position. It was a solid player with a defined market niche and the leading supplier of audiotex systems. The company had been profitable for thirteen consecutive quarters. Its voice directories systems were installed in more than

ninety markets worldwide, while its CITYLINE product offered information such as news and weather to thousands of callers around the world. In 1990, Brite earned national recognition when it was ranked number eighty-one on *Inc.* magazine's list of the one hundred fastest-growing small public companies.[32]

Yet it was clear to Brite, and any company in a high-tech or telecommunications field, that the future would not be easy. By the early 1990s, telecommunications had clearly become the linchpin on which corporate competitive success hinged. It was also clear that in spite of the technological advances occurring in telecommunications, the product that companies—and consumers—ultimately wanted to buy was not technology but rather the services that the technologies made possible. Therefore it became common for companies to merge their financial

Once its sales reached a certain volume, Brite grew extremely fast, selling audiotex systems to media companies around the world and expanding its product line into IVR applications and managed services.

and intellectual assets to create new entities that offered full-service solutions with enhanced competitive advantages.[33]

Brite's increasing reliance on Europe amplified the uncertainty. In August 1990, Probe Research recognized Brite for having the largest installed base of voice response of all the U.S. vendors marketing in Europe. But throughout the early 1990s, the fires of political change were raging across the Continent. Communism had imploded, new countries were rapidly organizing from the chaos of the former Soviet Union, and Germany was preparing for reunification. Brite, however, was determined to continue its overseas growth and saw more opportunity than risk. In August 1990, the company entered into a three-year agreement granting Infovox AB of Solna, Sweden, the right to manufacture and sell Brite products in Sweden and Norway.

"Infovox's reputation as a high-technology company and a leading provider of 'text-to-speech' systems is important to us," Brannan said. "Both of us work hard to provide after-the-sale support. This service philosophy is a key to winning new customers."[34]

Expanding Services

Despite the strong balance sheet and increasing sales, some analysts who followed the voice-processing market were quick to point out a potential weakness: Brite was vulnerable to competition from the increasing number of IVR and voice messaging vendors who were offering audiotex applications. As technology advanced, the cost of providing information systems was dropping dramatically. With less capital required to enter the market, small companies were rushing to create new niches for specific tasks based on new technologies.

To combat the new competition, Brite began expanding into market-specific information libraries that offered recurring revenue. Before, it had emphasized meeting the needs of media companies such as daily newspapers and television stations looking for a new way to generate additional revenue or an alternative medium to communicate with their audience. But by 1990 Brite had expanded its product line to include Gateway

One of Brite's original core products, the NewsLine. As competition increased in the audiotex industry, which included yellow pages, news services, and dating services, Brite began to move into other markets.

5000 for 800-number and 900-number service bureaus; Voice Directory for yellow-pages publishers and telephone companies; Real Estate Hotline for real estate brokers; CIN for cellular service providers; and Telecare for hospitals.[35]

A New Home

In the midst of this rapidly expanding market, Brite was also preparing to move its office. Relocation wasn't a new or even a very radical idea. Brannan had first raised the possibility in 1988 in an interview with the *Wichita Business Journal* when he remarked that Brite might relocate to Kansas City, where many sales meetings were held, or to the Southwest, where venture capital was more plentiful. While Wichita was a

beloved home for Brannan, it was a difficult place for a fledgling company to mature. The reasons included high airfares, lack of tax abatements for existing companies, and high property taxes on real estate.[36]

But as it turned out, Brite was still attached to its hometown. In March 1990, the company announced plans to move into a new, forty-thousand-square-foot headquarters at 739 East Twenty-first Street in Wichita. Its eighteen thousand square feet of office space was no longer adequate for a company with more than 116 people, a big jump from just 50 at the beginning of 1989.[37]

Buying VSG

In May 1991, further enhancing its global presence, Brite acquired the Voice Systems Group (VSG) of Ferranti Business Communications of Manchester, England, for $1,275,000. VSG, a leader in the European market for voice messaging products with 21 percent of installed ports, had twenty-nine employees in Manchester and two sales and technical support people in Wiesbaden, Germany.

"That acquisition came through a phone call I received," remembered Etherington. "Stan at first had no interest in it. But finally he had some people fly over and spend a couple days, including himself, Scott Walsh, and Don Mounday. We ended up buying the whole VSG."[38]

Operating after the acquisition as Brite Voice Systems Group Ltd. (BVSG), the new subsidiary quickly provided a substantial return on investment. Wiesbaden was convenient to many European centers of commerce and already supplied voice messaging systems to Austria, Switzerland, and other European countries through PBX distributors.

In addition, the new member of the Brite family had already delivered the two largest cellular voice messaging systems in the world, based on total subscribers served from a single system.[39] Both of these systems expanded significantly in 1991, leaving management optimistic about sales of the powerful cellular voice processing platforms in the future.

Brite's international presence was recognized in the December 1991 issue of *International*

Business magazine: it named the company the fifty-third–fastest-growing publicly owned company involved in international trade.[40]

Another international Brite success story that year was the completion of the initial Bell Canada Gateway System. Through its Canadian distributor, Time Communications, Brite, despite stiff competition, had been named vendor of choice in late 1990 by Canada's telephone monopoly. The system, part of a three-year contract with Bell Canada and its sister companies, was delivered during the fourth quarter of 1990 and first quarter of 1991.[41]

A Strategic Sea Change

In 1991, however, the situation changed rapidly once again. While Europe was still organizing new markets, the United States entered a steep recession. After a decade of strong growth and the successful prosecution of the Gulf War, many economists were surprised at how quickly America slipped into a recession. The impact was enormous, and for Brite it contained a lesson. So far, the company had made a living selling large systems to big companies. In the face of the recession and newly aggressive low-priced competition, however, Brite officers decided to reexamine their business model for new opportunities.

Their search was aided by an unlikely source: U.S. District Judge Harold H. Greene. On May 25, 1991, Greene lifted the information service ban on the seven Regional Bell Operating Companies (RBOCs). The ban, which had been in effect since the RBOCs were created in 1984, had prevented Brite from doing business with seven of the biggest corporations in the United States—companies that Brite considered some of its largest potential customers.[42]

"The recent court ruling that allowed the Regional Bell Operating Companies to offer talking yellow pages and other information services creates some very exciting opportunities for Brite," Brannan said in October 1991.[43]

Before long, company executives also decided to take a calculated risk. Brannan and Becky Splitt, general manager of Brite Communications Services, developed a 120-page business plan for an experiment with managed services. Instead of selling the hardware, which would have allowed Brite's customers to operate voice-mail systems on their own, a team of Brite employees would operate the systems in a joint venture with the customers. After the Brite board approved the plan, Splitt led a team of Brite employees to Columbus, Ohio, to launch the experiment in October 1991. It would be almost a year before the company could draw any conclusions about its foray into managed services.

Meanwhile, Brite targeted several key markets, including IVR and facsimile. The company introduced an interactive fax product that provided fax-on-demand and fax broadcasting services; and in April 1991 it announced the development of three new voice-processing units that could operate multiple voice-processing applications on the same platform.

In 1991, Brite made a profit of $1.23 million on revenues of $18 million. More than 40 percent of this revenue came from overseas sources.

The Brite Voice executive team. Clockwise from top left are Scotty Walsh, David Hemmings, Leon Ferber, and Glenn Etherington.

CHAPTER SIX

GAINING GROUND

1992–1998

We started a process of investigating. Instead of hiring a new CEO and starting this process of culture change all over again, should we consider merging with one of the major industry players who already had a management team in place with credentials and credibility?

—Stan Brannan

THE EARLY 1990S WERE A TIME OF transition for Brite Voice. The company had grown quickly, but it had also remained dependent on large-system sales—a risky proposition. Moreover, competition had begun to erode its basic market in the audiotex business, and the national economy dipped into a recession in 1991 and 1992.

In response to the changing climate, a Brite team had launched a managed-services experiment in Ohio in late 1991, devoting a year to forming partnerships with major corporations and selling managed services rather than single-system sales. It would take less than a year for Brite to begin benefiting from this strategy.

Staking Out International Markets

Before the managed-services strategy could yield many benefits, however, Brite faced more immediate concerns. The second quarter of 1992 proved to be one of the most difficult in Brite's history. In June, in response to weak domestic sales, Brite executives announced a reduction in staffing and recorded a related restructuring charge of approximately $800,000. To focus operations, the company also adopted the focused business unit (FBU) concept and reorganized into five areas: media, communication services, advanced technologies, international, and information systems.[1]

The communication services FBU was housed Brite's new managed-services operation, which had quickly proven that partnerships with customers could produce a steady stream of dependable revenue, a welcome contrast to the revenue roller coaster of large-system equipment sales.

Wall Street liked the reorganization, according to stock analyst Mark Scott, director of research for *Volume Investor*. "From the Wall Street perspective, it's an ideal strategy," he said. "Rather than sell a box for a one-time fee, they form a joint venture and share profits. Wall Street will pay a much higher multiple when earnings are reliable and less erratic."[2]

International sales remained the bright spot on Brite's balance sheet, representing 53 percent of the company's total revenues in 1992. BVSG, Brite's subsidiary in England and Germany, had an excellent year, rolling out the Voice Systems Director (VSD) in November. The VSD provided services such as voice mail, call completion, information services, and fax mail/distribution.[3]

The Brite VoiceSelect System product in the mid-1990s. Around this time, Brite adopted a new, focused business unit approach that concentrated on narrow markets.

Frank Trippi, left, director of international sales, and
Leon Ferber, executive vice president. Brite was a heavily
international company, with offices throughout the world.
Its prepaid wireless systems were a global standard.

To help sell the system, Brite expanded its
sales force in South and Central America, Asia
Pacific, central Europe, and the Middle East. It also
opened offices in Rome, Italy, and new distributors
were signed in Korea and Malaysia.[4]

The year would prove disappointing, however,
as revenue declined from $18 million in 1991 to
$17.5 million. Yet Brite had reason to hope that the
slump wouldn't last long. The managed-services
sector of its business continued to gain momentum—for the first quarter of 1993, its revenues
were $500,000. A new opportunity also appeared
as cellular communications continued to grow,
expanding the market for Brite's wireless voice
recognition product, VoiceTone Dialer. In March
1993, Brite announced its first VoiceTone Dialer
sale, to Metrocel Cellular Telephone Company in
Dallas. The sale portended many more.

Perception Technology

Like many companies its size, Brite was
always looking for good merger and acquisition
opportunities. In July 1993, hoping to gain larger
market share, Brite announced a merger with one
of its largest competitors, Perception Technology
Corporation, a provider of Interactive Voice
Response (IVR) systems.

"That was an interesting deal," recalled Brite
CFO Glenn Etherington.

*A vice president of Perception named Dan
Maitland called Stan and asked if there was a
way we could get together. So Scotty Walsh, Stan
Brannan, and I got into Stan's airplane and met
with Leon Ferber, Perception's CEO; Maitland; and
their CFO. We had a very nice half-day discussion,
and what happened was Leon Ferber pretty much
said, "I want to go back into the lab and be an engineer again. I don't want to be CEO of a public company." Then the CFO said, "I don't really want to
do this anymore, either." So he kind of ceded his
role to me. And Dan Maitland and Scotty Walsh
kind of paired their roles. At the end of the day,*

there was really very little political friction, and it made the transaction very easy.[5]

After the merger, Perception became Brite's sixth FBU. The Perception FBU provided voice response solutions to companies requiring sophisticated transaction processing applications. It allowed Brite to offer a full range of solutions, including audiotex, voice messaging, voice recognition, and IVR platforms.

To reduce redundancy and centralize operations, Perception's information services operation relocated to Wichita, Kansas, and purchasing and manufacturing facilities were centralized. Finally, the two companies' media and directory groups were combined into one business unit.[6]

The Perception merger resulted in a jump in revenue for 1993. Even after a $4.6 million charge, Brite reported a 32 percent increase in revenue.

The Pickup Begins

By 1994, the United States had emerged from its recession. Driven by the Internet, new communications technology, and booming worker productivity, the economy began its longest expansion in history. Over the next five years, the stock market would enter an unprecedented bull market, and the hottest sector would be technology. Yet even among the high-flying tech stocks of the 1990s, Brite stock was a standout. In January 1994, *Barron's* listed Brite stock as the fifteenth-largest percentage gainer for 1993 of all the companies listed on the NASDAQ stock market, and the twentieth-largest among stocks listed on the NYSE, AMEX, and NASDAQ.[7]

That year would in fact be Brite's most successful. Revenues for 1994 climbed 41 percent to $66.3 million, and the company achieved the highly coveted ISO 9001 certification in Europe and began working towards certification in the United States, which it would receive in 1997. System sales increased by about 40 percent, international sales jumped 46 percent, and managed-services revenue almost tripled, jumping from $3.5 million in 1993 to $9.3 million in 1994.[8] By the end of the year, Brite was debt free.

The *Kansas City Star* named Brite the region's top performer in 1994 for its 68.2 percent climb in stock value, among other feats.

The Wichita-based designer and manufacturer of voice processing systems turned in record earnings for the first three quarters of 1994, made a successful acquisition, and is a growing firm.[9]

The *Star* attributed Brite's remarkable success to three factors: its merger with Perception Technology, continued increases in system sales, and new emphasis on managed services.

System sales, which increased 34 percent, were driven by VoiceSelect, Brite's voice-activated dialing system for cellular telephones. At year-end, the product was in operation in thirty-four cities, and the company had installed multilingual systems in Canada, Puerto Rico, and Malaysia.[10]

Overseas, BVSG delivered its first Voice Systems Director (VSD) in late 1994, combining voice messaging, audiotex, and IVR in a single, scalable system. This milestone positioned Brite to become a significant provider to customers throughout Europe who required flexible, open systems.[11]

Yet no business showed as much raw potential as the managed-services FBU. In just two years, managed services had grown from nothing to revenues of nearly $1 million a month.[12] In many cases, managed services were generating annual revenues for Brite that exceeded the selling price of the basic system or technology.[13]

Scotty Walsh with his wife, Marie. He joined Brite Voice in 1990 as executive vice president and would be one of the few executives who remained with the company after the 1999 merger with InterVoice.

Brite finished 1994 with the largest backlog in its history. The company had successfully teamed up with six of the seven Regional Bell Operating Companies as well as GTE, Sprint, MCI, Intel, QVC, the *New York Times*, the *London Financial Times*, Tribune Newspapers, and many others.

Touch-Talk and TSL

Flush with cash, Brite continued shopping for like-minded companies. In 1995, the company completed three acquisitions: Touch-Talk in March; Internet Resources, a relatively small company that formed the basis of an Internet services division, in June; and four affiliated companies known as TSL in August.[14]

Touch-Talk was no stranger to Brite; it had developed custom software for Brite's IVR systems for several years. In fact, Touch-Talk had been the largest provider of customized application software used by Brite's IVR applications. Touch-Talk's software improved Brite's ability to support customers,

and Touch-Talk also provided tools that further automated Brite's software development process.

TSL was purchased in exchange for 3.331 million shares of common stock. The group comprised Telecom Services Limited (U.S.), Telecom Services Limited (West), TSL Software Services, and TSL Management Group. TSL offered an array of services and products that assisted clients in managing services like billing verification, operations management, technical consulting, and management software services.[15]

Both acquisitions—Touch Talk and TSL—were recorded as a pooling of interests, and Brite took a $4.3 million one-time charge. Revenues in 1995 jumped to a record $97.1 million, and if the one-time charge had been excluded, operating income and earnings per share would have reached record levels.[16]

Shrinking World, Expanded Market

Although international sales weren't its fastest-growing segment, there was no question that Brite was a global company. In 1995, international sales represented about a quarter of total revenue, and Brite technology was a leader throughout Asia and Europe. In the United Kingdom, Brite supplied voice mail technology for British Telecom/Cellnet. In Spain, it supplied a similar system for Telfonica.[17]

Much of this growth was due to strong sales of the Voice Systems Director (VSD). In the first full year of VSD sales, major markets opened in seven additional countries in Europe, Africa, and the Middle and Far East. In fact, Brite sold more voice mail system ports in Europe in 1995 than in the previous nine years and became the leading supplier to wireless networks in Africa and the Middle East. To aid its expansion, Brite opened new offices in 1995 in Singapore; Cambridge, England; and Johannesburg, South Africa.[18]

Meanwhile, VoiceSelect, Brite's voice dialing product, continued its dominance in the strong overseas wireless market. Brite now held the largest market share for voice-activated services in the global wireless-network marketplace.

Left: The Britelink system in the QVC Shopping Center phone banks in 1994. Like InterVoice, Brite sold IVR systems that helped reduce the human cost of answering thousands of similar phone calls.

Right: Mike Henrich, former president of Touch-Talk. Brite acquired Touch-Talk in 1995, gaining its expertise in custom software development for the telco industry.

Brannan's Honors

Much of the credit for Brite's success went to Stan Brannan, the driving force behind the company's strategy. In June 1995, Brannan was named "Entrepreneur of the Year" for Kansas and western Missouri as part of the National Entrepreneur of the Year awards program.[19]

It was well-deserved recognition. Brannan was once described as having the independent nature and confidence of a nineteenth century clipper captain—one who made bold yet studied business decisions and had the right dash of gumption for weathering stormy seas. His gift for developing pioneer services in the voice-processing market was matched only by his capacity to regroup and rechart under pressure. For example, when new regulations in Great Britain contributed to a 70 percent drop in international sales, Brite responded by seeking new markets in Sweden, Denmark, and Canada.

Yet Brannan never encouraged public adulation. Despite analyst coverage that frequently attributed Brite's enormous success directly to Brannan, he continued to push home the message that Brite's employees were the real wellspring. "People don't say Stan Brannan is great and the employees at Brite are lousy," he remarked. "They say, 'Brite Voice has quality people.'"[20]

Brite Prospects

By the mid-1990s, the days of the simple answering machine were gone forever. Telecommunications voice-processing systems were fast becoming staples in everyone's home, business, and automobile. In addition, both residential and business customers were discovering the advantage of voice-activated dialing services.

Brite Voice's products dovetailed perfectly with this new reality. As Brite's markets evolved, they were converging with other rapidly growing industries—including cable, media, Internet service providers, computer manufacturers, and software companies—creating an information "mega-market" that offered boundless opportunity. According to Frost & Sullivan, revenues for North American voice-processing services totaled $5.03 billion in 1995 and continued climbing, driven by computer-telephony integration and organizations' growing need for automated phone services twenty-four hours a day. Passage of the Telecommunications Act of 1996 spurred the competitive atmosphere, allowing companies of all types to offer long-distance and local telephone service as well as cable television service.

In just twelve short years, Brite had grown from five employees to 610. By 1996, sales had climbed to $93 million, and Brite had offices from San Francisco to New York and from Johannesburg to Hong Kong.[21] In Kansas, Brite occupied almost forty-eight thousand square feet of the former Mycro-Tek building at 9229 East Thirty-seventh Street North, in addition to a three-story headquarters on Twenty-first Street North in Wichita.

When technology stocks got hammered during early 1996 due to uncertainty in the market, many analysts insisted that Brite Voice still presented a good buy. Herbert Tinger, an analyst with First Albany, issued a buy recommendation in the summer of 1996—with a twelve-month target of $32 a share—because he believed the company was undervalued.

"Brite Voice is focused. A lot of competitors are too strongly focused on the sales side of the business, which is too unpredictable," said Tinger.[22] Tinger also hailed Brite's emphasis on the international market, which was growing at about 50 to 60 percent.

Mark Scott, an analyst who had followed the company since it went public, believed that Brite had done a much better job than Wall Street had ever given it credit for. "Stan [Brannan] is one of the best managers of the companies that I follow," Scott said. "He's one of the better visionaries."[23]

Howard Smith of First Analysis was also bullish on Brite, making it one of his top stock picks for 1996. "They got beat up pretty badly a couple of months ago for no apparent reason when other technology stocks got battered," he said in a February 1996 interview.[24]

The stock drop would not affect Brite's basic strategy. In early 1996, Brite—which already held more than 70 percent of the wireless voice-mail market in the United Kingdom—announced that it would offer voice and fax messaging services in the North American wireless market.[25]

Just one month later, Dallas-based Voice Control Systems announced that its speech

Top: An early 1990s Brite Voice cookout and watermelon party in the parking lot of its Wichita headquarters. Although it was growing quickly, Brite was a tight-knit company run by founder Stan Brannan and a small cadre of top executives.

Bottom: David Gergacz was hired in 1996 as president and CEO. Gergacz was a founding member of Sprint and quickly developed a strategic vision for his new company.

recognition technology—already used in Brite's VoiceSelect platform—had been installed by Ameritech Cellular Services and BellSouth Cellular. The cellular service providers were using VCS's speech recognition to provide hands-free voice dialing services in their wireless network. According to David Hemmings, executive vice president of Brite Voice, the partnership between the two industry leaders resulted in a 95 percent market share in the wireless industry worldwide.[26]

In August 1996, Brite signed the largest contract in its history. The order, from British Telecom Cellnet, represented a total commitment of about $18.6 million.[27]

Changing of the Guard

In December 1996, David Gergacz joined Brite as president and chief executive officer, replacing company founder Stan Brannan, who continued his role at Brite by focusing on new product development and acquisitions. A founder of Sprint, Gergacz was a CEO with a proven track record and deep experience in the telco industry. He had served as chief executive of Boston Technology, Canada's

Rogers Cantel, and Cincinnati Bell Telephone.[28]

Gergacz headed up an experienced team of telco industry veterans, including Gerald Butler, executive vice president of engineering and worldwide operations; Glenn Etherington, chief financial officer; Victoria Farris, vice president of finance; Stuart Hallam, chief executive for European operations; David Hemmings, executive vice

Stan Brannan, right, smiles as the CEO of Ohio Power Company signs a deal for Brite's IVR products.

president; Alan Maltz, executive vice president and director; and Scott Walsh, executive vice president of strategy and business development.

Gergacz quickly homed in on what he believed were Brite's three major market opportunities: enhanced services for the global telecommunications market; IVR and computer telephony integration for the corporate customer-service-automation market; and telecommunications management services for medium and large organizations.

His intent was to gain the majority of Brite's revenue from the enhanced services markets, which were predicted to grow at more than 30 percent annually.[29] This target extended overseas, where Brite hoped to increase the percentage of overseas revenues derived from managed services. Up till then, the vast majority of Brite's growth had come through sales of systems.

Brite was in a good position to fulfill Gergacz's vision. When he arrived, Brite and its subsidiaries had more than 700 employees, 505 of whom were located in the United States and 203 in Europe,

the Middle East, Africa, or Singapore.[30] The company posted record revenues of $110.4 million for 1996, up some 14 percent from $97.1 million.[31]

Betting on Prepaid

Along with managed services, Brite's move toward the prepaid wireless market proved to be a stroke of brilliance. The Yankee Group predicted that prepaid wireless would be a $2.2 billion industry with more than 2.7 million subscribers by 2002. Providers were running to the new market segment because, research had demonstrated, an estimated 20 to 30 percent of potential wireless subscribers had traditionally been turned away because of poor credit.[32] Prepaid was a perfect way to reach this large population.

By 1997, Brite, with more than 450,000 wireless subscribers worldwide, had made itself a clear market leader in prepaid calling.[33] It had secured both equipment and managed-services contracts from telco providers such as Ameritech, Cellular One, Radiofone, Wireless One, and Sprint PCS. In September 1997, Sprint PCS selected Brite to provide wireless prepaid services on Sprint's 100 percent digital, 100 percent PCS network. The two-year contract was the largest managed-services contract in Brite's history.[34]

Brite also regularly announced new wireless contracts around the world. Mobile network operators in Sweden, Turkey, Puerto Rico, Greece, Singapore, and Germany all signed large contracts for Brite products and services. By the end of the year, the company controlled 80 percent of the voice-activated dialing market worldwide, boasting pace-setting industry leaders such as AT&T Wireless, Ameritech, BellSouth, Rogers Cantel in Canada, Miniphone in Argentina, Telia in Sweden, and DDI and TDP in Japan.[35]

Glenn Etherington and his wife, Chier Hunter. Etherington joined Brite in 1988 as chief financial officer and was instrumental in arranging the InterVoice merger.

A Global Corporate Headquarters

In mid-1997, Gergacz made the decision that Brannan had flirted with previously: he decided to move Brite out of Wichita. But instead of Kansas City, Gergacz had a different place in mind. He announced that Brite would relocate to Orlando, Florida.[36]

He had several reasons for such a drastic move. First of all, Brite had outgrown Kansas. Second, Florida had tax advantages and Orlando had offered $1.5 million in further tax credits to Brite. Most importantly, the new location would house a centralized management team and was more convenient to Brite's East Coast telecommunications and banking customers—as well as the burgeoning European market.[37] Within a few months, Brite had about eighty employees in a new forty-thousand-square-foot Orlando headquarters.

Obviously, Brite's culture was dramatically affected by the change in leadership and the move. It was, Brannan noted, the end of the "Stan Brannan family."[38] Nevertheless, the core of Brite's senior management, including Scotty Walsh and Glenn Etherington, relocated. Ray Naeini also moved, and he was given responsibility for global network services and systems shortly afterward. Brite chairman Stan Brannan, however, had no plans to relocate. Instead, he announced he would travel frequently between Kansas and Florida.[39]

Although Brite was doing well, the move had financial consequences. In the second quarter of 1997, Brite recorded a $7.3 million loss. Gergacz, however, announced that he was pleased with Brite's performance in several areas, particularly its network systems business, which had increased more than 50 percent from the previous year.[40]

Gergacz's next move was a step toward his long-range vision for Brite Voice. In late 1997, Brite sold its electronic publishing business for $35 million to IT Network, a telephone subsidiary of Source Media. While the electronic publishing business had proved itself profitable—generating $11.2 million at the end of 1997—management believed that its growth prospects were limited.[41]

Without Wires

The wireless market, however, more than made up for the loss. In 1997, the Yankee Group predicted that annual revenue from enhanced

The lab at Brite's East Twenty-first Street North location in Wichita. After Brite moved its headquarters to Orlando, the product development team and Brannan stayed in Wichita.

wireless services would increase more than seven-fold in the United States—from $98 million in 1997 to $773 million by 2002.[42]

In December 1997, Brite signed a $25 million agreement with AT&T to provide enhanced tele-communications products. It was the largest con-tract in the company's history, leading Brite Voice Vice President Scotty Walsh to remark that "they were good times."[43] The full scope of the deal was truly staggering: Over the life of the four-year contract, the deal would be worth an estimated $50 million to $80 million.[44]

Brite's disappointing financial results for 1997—a 9 percent increase in revenue to $119.8 million[45]—were generally attributed to the company's transi-tion. Some consolation came from one key accomplishment: the consolidation of its systems around an open architecture called BriteESP. In the next year, Brite would build on that founda-tion with the introduction of several feature-rich products, including BriteTalk for voice-activated dialing, BriteDebit for prepaid wireless calling, and BriteConnect, a flexible platform for IVR and CTI services that *CTI Magazine* named "Product of the Year."[46]

Stan Brannan Resigns

In April 1998, Gergacz, already CEO and president, was named chairman of the board,

CREATIVE RECRUITING

IN THE BUSINESS WORLD, IT ISN'T unusual for companies to try to steal workers away from their rivals. But Brite Voice took a different tack when it turned to one of its best customers—AT&T—to help fill new jobs.

Brite put out a call in April 1998 for about two hundred high-tech employees to fill openings at the new headquarters in central Florida. At about the same time, AT&T Chairman Michael Armstrong announced plans to pare down the size of his company's workforce by about eighteen thousand nationwide. AT&T had about five thousand employees in central Florida at the time.

With the common goal of keeping high-tech jobs in the region, the two firms joined forces and held a recruiting fair at Brite headquarters in which about 150 AT&T employees dropped by to learn more about Brite and discuss job prospects. "We talked about it and thought it made sense. We like their people. We like their skills," said Brian Klumpp, Brite's senior vice president for human resources.[1]

The two companies came up with the slogan "There's a Brite career after AT&T."[2]

succeeding Stan Brannan. Brannan resigned for personal reasons: His twenty-one-year-old son, Christopher, had been mugged and stabbed, and Brannan wanted time to tend to his son.

"I know David Gergacz and the Brite management team will continue to guide the company to new success," Brannan announced to the financial press. "My personal focus must be with my wife to help care for Chris and get him through an extended period of rehabilitation."[47]

Despite Brannan's departure, the company continued to perform well. On June 2, 1998, Brite stock spiked to a fifty-two-week high. During a CNBC interview, market guru Joe Granville, editor of the *Granville Market Letter*, called Brite "the best stock on NASDAQ" and predicted it would trade as high as $22 in six to twelve months.[48]

Asian Economic Turmoil Subsides

Meanwhile, market strategy was taking on a whole new meaning for wireless carriers in Asia Pacific, where an epidemic financial crisis was beginning to abate. Throughout the early 1990s, the so-called tiger economies of Thailand, Korea, Taiwan, Singapore, Indonesia, and Malaysia had grown at breathtaking rates. In 1997, however, the entire region plunged into a fierce recession. Its previously thriving high-technology markets almost evaporated.

By 1999, many of these countries were beginning to stage mild recoveries, and telco carriers were looking at ways to maintain or even increase their subscriber bases.[49] Brite's prepaid products were particularly attractive in such a region. In September 1998, in a deal valued at more than $15 million, one of the largest wireless carriers in Asia Pacific selected Brite to provide advanced voice-activated dialing services.[50]

Another important achievement in 1998 was the reorganization of its Europe, Middle East, Africa (EMEA) operation. Over the years, acquisitions of multiple companies with different technological platforms and administrative methods had created inefficiencies in EMEA that pinched Brite's performance. By year-end, however, EMEA had returned to profitability and won several important new contracts.

The Months before the Merger

In November 1998, David Gergacz, president, CEO, and chairman, resigned from Brite, taking analysts by surprise. Herbert Tinger, with First Albany in New York, said the management change appeared to be an issue of differences over management style rather than substance. "Gergacz did a good job of restructuring the company . . . and now that it's done, they're looking for the next step," Tinger said.[51]

That next step included company founder Brannan, who returned as interim CEO while a nationwide search for new leadership began. Of course, this search would be suspended permanently by the merger with InterVoice, which was less than a year in the future.

"We started a process of investigating," Brannan said. "Instead of hiring a new CEO and starting this process of culture change all over again, should we consider merging with one of the major industry players who already had a management team in place with credentials and credibility?"[52]

Company executives agreed. "We had no doubt that we would make our business plan and that we would achieve the growth rates we wanted if we stayed by ourselves," remembered Brite Voice Vice President Scotty Walsh. "However, we thought that the shareholders would be better off and that we could take it further with the combined companies rather than stand alone."[53]

Above: Ray Naeini, vice president of Advanced Technology, with his wife, Shahin. Naeini was one of the Brite executives who moved from Wichita to Orlando.

Left: Stan Brannan and his wife, Sue. Brannan remained in Kansas after the move but was a frequent flier between the two cities. When Gergacz resigned in 1998, Brannan became interim CEO while the company looked at its options.

In the meantime, the company continued to streamline and focus its business on its most profitable segments. In November 1998, Brite Voice announced the sale of its TSL division for $25 million.[54] Henceforth, Brite would rely on managed services, overseas sales (of both equipment and managed services), and the wireless market. "We positioned ourselves in the market as value-added services," said Naeini, executive vice president of global products. "We were in prepaid, in voice-activated applications, and in voice messaging."[55]

By any indication, Brite's strategy was a winner: the company closed the books on 1998 with revenue of $135.7 million, a 13 percent year-over-year increase.[56] "Remembering that our business is selling to telephone companies, I believe there is more demand than we can keep up with and that we will continue to experience significant growth," said Executive Vice President Scotty Walsh.[57]

Over the next year, new agreements and contracts were announced seemingly on a weekly basis. In January, Voice Control Systems, a leader in natural speech recognition, signed a multiyear agreement with the company to supply large-vocabulary speech recognition capabilities.[58] Brite also sold technology systems in Germany, Japan, and throughout Asia Pacific.

Driven by new sales, Brite crossed a major threshold when it announced that the number of worldwide subscribers using its prepaid services exceeded two million. More than one million of those subscribers used prepaid wireless through Brite's managed-service solutions.

"The two million global subscriber milestone is important because it demonstrates the strong market demand for the convenience, flexibility and affordability that our prepaid services bring to wireless services," said Naeini.[59]

All of this euphoria took place, of course, against the backdrop of the impending merger with Inter-Voice. Negotiated by Brannan with his counterpart at InterVoice, Dan Hammond, the merger had the enthusiastic support of senior executives at both companies. It promised to be a perfect fit—the companies had complementary technology, markets, and even strategies.

"The last few years have been incredibly challenging—both externally and internally—because the corporation has gone through so many changes," Naeini remarked. "We changed the CEO and the chairman. We moved the headquarters. We changed organizations. We did the merger. We reorganized," he said.

I enjoyed it tremendously because I felt I was part of a team that took an organization which had done barely $12 million in revenue in the network environment to the point we're at today, where we're running over $160 million—and that's all happened in just four or five years.[60]

PART III

I N 1999, LEADERS FROM BOTH COMPA-
nies, InterVoice and Brite Voice Systems,
announced the acquisition of Brite by
InterVoice. With the stroke of a pen, a new
company, InterVoice-Brite, would be born.
Overnight, the IVR industry would have a
new leader.

Three years later, in 2002, the new company stood on the threshold of a new age. The
technology was rapidly evolving, and the lines
between previously separate data streams had
all but disappeared.

In the technological world of the future,
billions of people would be connected to the
Internet, often with wireless technologies,
and data and video would ride the information highway with impunity. The goal
was total connectivity, any time, anywhere,
for everybody.

InterVoice-Brite would play an important
role in this future. There seemed little doubt
that the standard click-and-scroll screen and
QWERTY keyboard would soon be relegated to
history's attic. In their places would stand fully
empowered, artificially intelligent machines
that could understand and respond to the
complete spectrum of human speech. On that
day, InterVoice-Brite, a company with a long
history of innovation, would finally see its long-
term vision realized.

Stan Brannan, CEO of Brite Voice Systems, and Dan
Hammond, CEO of InterVoice, at the signing that united
their two companies.

The formal offer by InterVoice to acquire Brite Voice. Brite's board accepted this offer rather than hire a new CEO.

CHAPTER SEVEN

THE INTERVOICE-BRITE MERGER

We were speaking the same language from the very first meeting.

—Stan Brannan

THE ACQUISITION OF BRITE Voice by InterVoice was a seminal moment in both companies' histories. Indeed, it was a seminal moment for the entire IVR industry.

Before the acquisition, the companies were very different organizations, based in different cities and selling different products to very different markets. Whereas InterVoice had spent the previous decade formalizing its processes and developing standards, Brite had remained a relatively informal company run by a core group of executives. And at the same time that InterVoice had become a leader in the domestic IVR equipment market, Brite had evolved into a leader in the global managed-services, voice mail, and wireless arenas.

Yet management viewed many of these differences as strengths, as if the companies were opposite sides of the same coin. With complementary technology platforms and markets and nearly the same size, both companies stood to gain a tremendous amount by joining.

The Original Discussions

InterVoice and Brite Voice were not new to each other. Executives at the two companies had discussed the possibility of "doing something together" intermittently since the 1980s, but nothing serious developed. Even up until 1998, before David Gergacz left Brite, the two companies were in periodic discussions regarding a merger, remembered Brite CFO Glenn Etherington, but "not much happened."

"I think it wasn't positioned particularly well and we didn't really know who was going to do what," Etherington remembered. "But then David Gergacz left in the fall of 1998, and I received a message from Stan Brannan that InterVoice was interested in talking again."[1]

This time, talks were serious, and Brite was a motivated player. Over the previous two years, the company had changed its CEO, moved its headquarters, and undergone significant employee turnover. Of the original Brite Voice, a core group of executives remained in Orlando, a group of software developers operated in Kansas, and a large group worked in the Manchester, England, office.

Brannan was a major motivating factor. When he came back to the company he founded, the interim CEO kept his options open. At the same time that Brannan was conducting a nationwide search for a new CEO, he was considering merger or acquisition partners. It was also a reasonable time for Brite to consider joining forces with another

Stan Brannan, left, shakes hands with Dan Hammond, right, to consummate the acquisition of Brite Voice by InterVoice.

company: The industry was experiencing a period of consolidation at the same time Brite was without a CEO. A merger or acquisition not only would benefit Brite shareholders; if it were a strategic fit, it would also enhance the company's position in its industry.

"There was a simultaneous process," Brannan remembered. "We interviewed CEOs, and we contacted people in the industry we felt would be potential partners for a merger. We contacted three or four players, including InterVoice, and went through several meetings of the management teams. Inter-Voice was very interested in Brite because our products and markets were new markets for them, and there was a minimum of overlap or redundancy."[2]

From InterVoice's side, the move didn't necessarily start out as an acquisition of an equally sized company. During the original round of conversations, remembered InterVoice Chief Financial Officer Rob-Roy Graham, management was thinking about a merger, or from an accounting standpoint, a pooling of interests.

"But as we began to look at the stock values of each company, we thought, at the time, it might be more beneficial to all the shareholders of Brite and to the former InterVoice to do it as a purchase using cash as primary currency," Graham said.[3] InterVoice also had indications from Bank of America that the bank would provide a loan to cover the complete acquisition. Although it was more debt than Dan Hammond liked to carry, Inter-Voice had strong cash flow.

Based on InterVoice's undervalued stock, the loan offer, and Brite's CEO situation, InterVoice

management made a decision: instead of a pooling of interests, the move would be positioned as a purchase. Right around the same time that Brannan was presenting CEO candidates to the board, InterVoice made its offer. The Brite board looked at its options and picked InterVoice.

As it turned out, after the offer was made, the financial picture changed because of internal Bank of America circumstances. The bank was moving much of its Texas-based decision making to its high-tech practice in California. When the California group's evaluation of the proposal came back, the bank offered to finance 75 percent of the transaction value through a bank loan. The rest of the price was to be paid with InterVoice stock.

On April 27, 1999, InterVoice and Brite Voice Systems announced the acquisition. Based on approximately 12.3 million Brite shares outstanding, the total cost to InterVoice was about $164.4 million.[4] In the newly combined company, the management ranks would look familiar, drawing on the experience of both companies—although Inter-Voice executives would still hold the top positions. Dan Hammond remained chairman and CEO and Stan Brannan would serve on the InterVoice-Brite board of directors as vice chairman. Senior

---

The InterVoice exhibit, InterAction, at the annual VCS distributor conference. Myra Hambleton, wearing a blue shirt, talks with potential customers. VCS was one of the industry's premier voice companies and a supplier to InterVoice.

members of the new company's management team included David Berger as president and chief operating officer; Rob-Roy Graham as chief financial officer; and Ray Naeini and Scotty Walsh as executive vice presidents.

"Merging InterVoice and Brite makes a lot of sense," said Brannan. "The combined marketing, customer support, and product development organizations should produce better long-term growth and success. I am excited about my role as vice chairman, and I expect to work very hard to make sure the anticipated benefits of this merger are achieved for customers, employees and shareholders."[5]

In mid-August, InterVoice announced that it had completed its merger with Brite Voice Systems and planned to change its name to InterVoice-Brite at the upcoming shareholders meeting.[6] Five days later, the amendment to the articles of incorporation was officially approved, and the new company changed its name to InterVoice-Brite Inc. InterVoice's ticker symbol (INTV) remained unchanged.[7]

Strength in Numbers

With the stroke of a pen, the new company, InterVoice-Brite, had become the world's leading supplier of high-tech call automation hardware and services for both corporate and telecommunications markets.[8] The company posted annual revenues of approximately $273 million and had a combined research and development budget of about $35 million. It was an ISO 9001–certified manufacturing corporation that employed about fourteen hundred, held thirty-eight patents, and had satellite offices in the Americas, Europe, Asia, and Africa. The company was active in more than sixty-five countries, and its client list included Ericsson, AT&T, Sprint PCS, E*TRADE, and Ford Credit.

"With this merger, there is clearly a leader in the field of call automation," said Hammond. "Separately, the companies had complementary technologies and markets, which means the new company is well positioned to serve the global call automation market."[9]

The acquisition made immediate sense to the financial press. InterVoice had about 70 percent of its business in banks and enterprise systems and the remaining 30 percent in networks and telcos. Brite's sales were exactly the opposite: about 70 percent network and 30 percent enterprise. As one

executive put it, InterVoice products saved money for customers by reducing the need for operators while Brite's product made money by offering value-added service such as prepaid wireless and voice mail. Both companies had experience with customer transactions and IVR, network applications, value-added services, and complex network integration.

The *Wichita Eagle* called the merger "almost a merging of twins: Both Brite and InterVoice make and install enhanced telecommunications systems and interactive information systems; both had similar earnings last year; and both have about seven hundred employees."[10]

The Culture Question

Although the product and business mix was a perfect, complementary fit, the integration of the two cultures would be a delicate process that fell heavily on Don Brown, InterVoice vice president, human resources.

"With the merger, we basically doubled the size of the company," Brown said. "It was a significant challenge for human resources because these two companies had two different cultures and ways of doing business. Everything they did, it seems like, was diametrically opposed."[11]

While InterVoice and Brite had both built world-class teams of computer-telephony professionals, they had evolved unique cultures. In the former InterVoice, decisions were made more throughout the organization with a participative management style. Because of the diffuse responsibility, it sometimes took longer to make decisions and required more paperwork and legal oversight. At Brite, in contrast, most of the decisions were made by the four top executives—Stan Brannan, Glenn Etherington, Scotty Walsh, and Ray Naeini—and handed down to the organization. It was faster but less formal and more autocratic. It was a telling example of the companies' differences that Brite had no on-staff legal counsel and no formal patent program while InterVoice had both. Combining the two, remarked Brown, would "require a tremendous amount of communication from management."[12]

Within these broad frameworks lurked countless small merger details. For example, the new organization would have to decide how to approach employees who remained loyal to their own products, their own cultures and rituals, and even their own offices. There was also the question of downsizing as redundant positions were eliminated.

Kathy Hackney, manager of human resources at InterVoice, found herself on the front line once again, traveling around the country to Brite offices to explain the migration of benefits and the strategy for combining the companies. "When it was announced, employees on both sides were concerned about redundant jobs being cut back," Hackney said. "So it's been my role to go out to the U.S.-based employees of Brite, into their offices, and present the plan. Everybody from Brite was very warm, very receptive."[13]

Rob-Roy Graham, InterVoice CFO, remembered that the acquisition proceeded very quickly once the decision was made to move forward. He remained CFO of the new company.

Geography was also an issue. Brite had about one hundred employees—mainly software engineers—in its Wichita office, another two hundred in the Orlando headquarters, and a manufacturing facility in Canton, Massachusetts.[14] Overseas, the company had a office in Manchester, England, with three hundred employees and operated satellite offices around the world. InterVoice, by contrast, did business almost totally out of Dallas.

Plans were made to shut the Canton facility and transfer Brite's Orlando headquarters operation to Dallas, meaning that executives like Scotty Walsh and Ray Naeini, who had moved to Florida less than two years before now had to face another relocation. Once again, Brite experienced personnel attrition: Of the entire Orlando staff, only Walsh and Naeini completed the move. The Wichita office, where Brite's software designers worked, was to remain open for the immediate future. In all, several hundred employees were offered termination packages in the months immediately after the merger.

The Street Reacts

To some extent, these issues are normal in any acquisition, and Wall Street's reaction was favorable to both the strategy to merge the companies and the broader philosophy behind the acquisition.

"First, the combination of the two companies creates a much larger entity that will be in a much stronger position to contest for larger contracts," declared a Piper, Jaffray research paper.

Brite Voice, for example, has been in the running for $50 million annual contracts—significant considering the company achieved revenues of $135 million for all of 1998. As a larger entity, the chance of success in winning these contracts only increases.

The larger size will better position InterVoice, given that it has seen a growing number of customer prospects wishing they could turn to a de facto leader as their supplier. The IVR market is highly fragmented. Dataquest estimates that InterVoice has a 12 percent market share—while Brite Voice possesses an 8 percent share. The combined entity will own 20 percent of the IVR market—almost twice the share of the next competitor.[15]

This potential, coupled with the cost savings, led the analyst firm to rate InterVoice-Brite a "strong buy" with a twelve-month target of $20 per share, up from the low teens.[16]

Analysts also took note that the merger alleviated two concerns shadowing InterVoice: a reliance on big-ticket premise equipment and a potential sales bubble from Y2K upgrades. The acquisition lessened the dependence on premises-based IVR sales—which dropped from 80 percent to 50 percent of revenue—and provided a recurring source of managed-services revenue.[17]

While most financial analysts believed that the sale would strengthen both companies' bottom lines, there was some criticism regarding the "low" price InterVoice had paid, and a few industry watchers commented that Brite Voice management was selling the company for much less than it was worth.[18] The $164.4 million price was slightly more than Brite's fiscal year 1998 revenues. Some analysts considered a range of around three times annual revenue to be more advisable.[19]

Operational Synergies

As it turned out, even the most optimistic expectations fell short when it came to the immediate financial impact of the acquisition. InterVoice-Brite had initially estimated it would save $20 million to $25 million in reduced costs and increased sales opportunities, but it was a modest prediction.

Because InterVoice hardware was an industry leader, the company immediately began to migrate Brite Voice's customers, which had previously used third-party hardware, to InterVoice hardware. This was an effort, remembered Graham, that saved between $10 million and $15 million annually in about fifteen minutes.[20]

It was also the first major test of the companies' combined potential, and it wasn't without challenges. "We were expecting to continue the InterVoice line on the enterprise side because it had the

Dan Hammond became CEO of a company with some $300 million in global revenue and a network of offices that reached around the globe.

more dominating market share," remembered Ray Naeini. "We had some setbacks regarding the former Brite's enterprise customers in that process, but [by early 2002] the revival was happening."[21]

Dwain Hammond, an InterVoice vice president, remembered that many of the Brite enterprise customers were "not happy about it at first" when it came to switching products. "Over time, those folks have come back, and they're evaluating InterVoice against the rest of the competition," he said. "We had to go in and spend weeks and weeks just looking at how we come up with a product migration plan so we can take care of the installed base and show them that the product direction is a good one for them."[22]

Similarly, Brite immediately adopted InVision, InterVoice's development tool, which was "one of the best in the industry and has been one of the best for a long time," said Gordon Givens, vice president, business systems operations and services.[23]

At the same time Brite was converting to InterVoice hardware, it was also absorbing InterVoice's much smaller managed-services, or application service provider (ASP), business. Over the years, Brite had built up a huge and rapidly growing managed-services operation that worked with global telecommunications giants such as British Telecom and Sprint PCS. In November, only three months after the acquisition was final, InterVoice-Brite extended its prepaid services contract with BT/Cellnet, signing a new agreement that was valued at more than $75 million over two and a half years.[24]

"It was a revolution for me," remembered Walt Mirkowicz, an InterVoice manager on the network side who migrated into Brite's network operation after the merger. "It was a huge change in perspective."[25]

Moreover, InterVoice's large pool of existing enterprise customers represented a new market for ASP services. These businesses, which had been using InterVoice systems for years, were becoming receptive to signing a managed-service contract because it allowed them to stay on the leading edge without having to make a large up-front investment.

When these benefits—swapping services and technology among formerly separate customer bases—were realized, executives at the new InterVoice-Brite estimated the company had benefited by about $25 million.

Similar complementary strengths flowed from the companies' geographic distributions. In a broad sense, Brite was an international company while InterVoice was a domestic one. Brite, with an established foothold in Europe and the United Kingdom, actually drew the lion's share of its revenue from outside the United States. InterVoice, on the other hand, had experienced success in Latin America.[26]

"We got what we were looking for," Graham said. "In Europe, we were always trying to find the distribution channel to take our high-margin products, and we had some difficulty in establishing those channels. When we found Brite, those channels were already there, and it became easier to approach the marketplace."[27]

Brite's Manchester office became the overseas headquarters for the new company.

The Industry Responds

Even before the full benefits of the acquisition were realized, InterVoice-Brite was earning recognition. In September, Cahners In-Stat Group identified InterVoice-Brite as the number one supplier of IVR systems to both the United States and the global market. "InterVoice's continued market leadership is testament to the company's commitment to leading-edge technology development, to technology integration capabilities, and to their customers," said Paul Stockford, director of voice and data communications for Cahners In-Stat Group. "The recent merger with Brite Voice Systems will also be instrumental in further expanding the InterVoice international presence in the future."[28]

According to In-Stat, the domestic market for IVR systems during 1998 was approximately 1.3 billion end-user revenues, and the worldwide market was approximately $1.7 billion end-user revenues.[29]

InterVoice-Brite next won C@ll Center CRM Solutions magazine's 1999 Product of the Year award for its OneVoice IVR platform. Frost & Sullivan

In 2000, the newly merged InterVoice-Brite suffered a downturn. In response, David Brandenburg returned to his old company as CEO and instituted a reorganization.

selected InterVoice-Brite as 1999 winner of the Marketing Engineering Leadership Award. And, for the second year in a row, the editors of *Telecom Business* magazine recognized InterVoice-Brite as one of the most influential and leading-edge companies in the telecommunications industry.[30]

Hitting a Bump

In early 2000, as InterVoice-Brite was still working through the issues of integrating the two companies, it received an unpleasant surprise. Although the acquisition was widely seen as good strategy, InterVoice-Brite missed its first-quarter earnings expectations because the Y2K readiness frenzy had ended.

There were many other reasons, too. The telecommunications industry, after experiencing double-digit growth throughout the 1990s, was finally beginning to slow. At the same time, the sales function at InterVoice needed to expand once again, and the sales force was being retrained. In June 2000, Dan Hammond and CFO Rob-Roy Graham faced the unpleasant task of informing analysts that InterVoice was going to miss its earnings targets. Predictably, the reaction was unpleasant. Within two days, InterVoice stock had dropped almost 55 percent to $6.13 a share.[31]

Developments followed with alacrity. First, Dan Hammond decided to step down. He had been CEO for fifteen years and persevered through numerous stock and business cycles, and he had realized his personal goal of taking the company to $250 million in revenue. He placed a call to his old friend and fellow board member David Brandenburg, asking if he would return to the company as CEO. "It was a real quick deal," Brandenburg remembered. "I think I got a call on Thursday night. I talked to a couple board members and talked to Dan about how it would happen. I think by Saturday, my decision was, 'Yes. I'll do it.' It was announced on Monday, and we had our shareholder meeting on Wednesday."[32]

On June 26, 2000, the company publicly announced that David Brandenburg would replace Hammond as chief executive officer, while Hammond would continue as chairman of the board. Hammond wouldn't hold this position long; by December, he would step down as chairman of the board also.[33]

It was an amicable transition, one that was carefully considered by the executives involved, all of whom were old colleagues and friends. Wall Street, which had so recently punished InterVoice-Brite for its missed quarters, was pleased. Besides being a known quantity, David Brandenburg commanded the respect of analysts and competitors alike.

In his first weeks, Brandenburg surveyed the company and came to the familiar conclusion that it needed to add more salespeople. Beyond this, he had no immediate plans to restructure the company. The downturn, he thought, was a temporary condition caused mainly by Y2K buying patterns. "My goal was as much as possible to keep the team in place and make changes based on what I observed, but not any big changes," Brandenburg said.

Over the course of the year, however, as he continued talking to people throughout the company, he came to the conclusion that InterVoice-Brite needed more serious change than he had thought and that the industry's problems ran deeper than Y2K orders drying up. "Things didn't feel quite right," Brandenburg said. "By the end of the third quarter, I had made some decisions that we had to make some major changes."[34]

In taking this position, InterVoice-Brite was one of the first companies in its industry to fully recognize the oncoming recession of early 2001. In preparation, the company reduced worldwide staff by about 12 percent, or one hundred positions. The most drastic change, though, had to do with the ongoing assimilation of the two very different businesses. Even after a year, it was clear that the former InterVoice and the former Brite Voice would have difficulty merging seamlessly into one another. Their customers, technologies, and cultures were simply too far apart.

"When we first combined," remarked Gordon Givens, "there was a big feeling that we were just going to put everything together in one big pile and go at both markets. I think that really confused the marketplace."[35]

The confusion wasn't limited to the marketplace; the two organizations in fact had very little contact.

"We don't overlap all that much," said Myra Hambleton, a software engineer from InterVoice. "We're very product-centric in the enterprise side, and the telco market is very custom-centric. That makes us very, very different in the way we do things. My operations staff doesn't want to touch things that are not released, but the telco side of the house—they're more familiar with customization."[36]

New Organizational Structure

To deal with the disparities, Brandenburg announced a major restructuring at InterVoice-Brite near the end of 2000. In actuality, it wasn't a formal restructuring so much as an acknowledgment of the company's reality, but it represented a major shift in strategy nonetheless. InterVoice-Brite was going to be split into two autonomous divisions, each with sales, marketing, research and development, operations, and customer service functions and its own general manager. Manufacturing, however, would be centralized.

The new Networks Systems Division, which essentially comprised Brite's operation, was headed up by Executive Vice President Ray Naeini. The new Enterprise Systems Division, which corresponded to the old InterVoice, would be led by Executive Vice President Bob Ritchey, who was hired expressly to run this business. Both Naeini and Ritchey reported to president and chief operating officer David Berger, although Berger himself would leave the company only a few months after the announcement.[37]

Both inside and outside InterVoice-Brite, there was a general consensus that this was the best way to organize the businesses. "Everybody had really rallied around the new divisions," Brandenburg said. "They have taken them seriously, giving the divisions total responsibility for profit and loss."[38]

The Future Is Now

In fiscal year 2000, InterVoice-Brite was the industry leader, with sales of approximately $323 million (including Brite's first quarter figures).[39] Yet while the company's market leadership was clear, so was its challenge. The rapid pace of technological development had not slowed while InterVoice-Brite worked through its acquisition issues. Natural speech recognition was closer to actuality than ever before, and the world's various telecommunications platforms were converging. Wireless and cellular communication continued to explode in popularity, especially in the developing world. As a combined company, InterVoice-Brite was positioned better than either of its former halves, but management was keenly aware of the task ahead.

The InterVoice-Brite lab in Dallas. By 2002, InterVoice-Brite was a leader in voice processing hardware and software.

CHAPTER EIGHT

TECHNOLOGY TALKS

1999–2001

*We've always been a good technology company. In the future, we're
going to keep that legacy, but we're really going to emphasize sales
and marketing.*

—David Brandenburg, 2002

INTERVOICE-BRITE WASN'T THE ONLY company to miss a few quarters in 2000. After double-digit growth through the mid- and late 1990s, the telecommunications and information technology industries generally weakened in the new millennium.

It was a sudden decline but not a surprise. Between 1997 and 1999, the telecommunications industry had grown at 12 percent annually, thanks to deregulation and rapid globalization.[1] Yet these same forces had resulted in severe pricing pressure on the long-distance market. Meanwhile, wireless technology and the Internet were developing rapidly, causing companies to invest billions to build high-speed Internet and digital cellular networks.[2] Infrastructure spending jumped by almost 30 percent annually.[3]

The rationale behind this explosive development was simple. Leaders in the telecommunications industry envisioned a day when one company could offer everything: wireless, high-speed Internet, long distance, cable, and even local phone service. By early 2000, however, indications surfaced that this vision might not be realized quickly. Consumers weren't responding the way the industry had expected. Broadband Internet access didn't take off as quickly as had been predicted, and hundreds of millions of dollars worth of newly installed fiberoptic cable was severely underutilized. Meanwhile, local phone competition had all but disappeared as the RBOCs merged and tightened control in the markets. Finally, voice-over Internet protocol (VoIP) technology didn't materialize as fast as some industry watchers had expected.

"Investors initially thought the opportunities were so immense and wide open that any company stood a good chance of reaping a windfall as long as the company had its bucket underneath the spigot," said Elliott Hamilton, senior vice president of the Strategis Group.[4]

In 2000, the good times ended. Almost simultaneously, all three of the United States's top long-distance carriers—AT&T, WorldCom, and Sprint— announced plans to pull back from the market. Their stocks plunged, and between March and September, the three lost roughly two-thirds of their market capitalization.[5]

Facing double-digit declines in long-distance revenue, AT&T announced in October 2000 that it would once again break apart. Chief Executive C. Michael Armstrong predicted there would be three companies by 2002: AT&T Business, AT&T Wireless, and AT&T Broadband. The dwindling

Heading into the future, telecommunications networks would continue to represent about half of InterVoice-Brite's revenue. The rest would come from traditional enterprise customers.

consumer long-distance segment would be a segment of AT&T Business.[6]

WorldCom followed suit a week after AT&T's announcement, saying it would separate its long-distance business, MCI, with separate stock. And just days later, Sprint shifted its business focus from long distance to the increasingly competitive data services market.[7]

This sudden downturn in telecommunications stock and availability of capital—combined with InterVoice-Brite's internal restructuring—all contributed to the company's missed quarters. Yet newly appointed CEO David Brandenburg was reading the future correctly: the downturn would be temporary. Unfortunately, it would last much longer than anyone expected.

The year had its bright spots, however. In January 2000, InterVoice-Brite won the prestigious Product of the Year award from *C@ll Center CRM Solutions* magazine for its OneVoice platform, marking the second consecutive year it had received the honor. The previous year, InterVoice had won for its AgentConnect call center platform.[8] AgentConnect received further accolades in July 2000, when it

was named Best of Show at the Communications Solutions EXPO in spring of 2000.

Speech Recognition Takes Off

According to most company insiders, the future lay with a newly realized technology—one that InterVoice-Brite had been working on for more than a decade. Since the first computers, engineers had been working toward the day when a human could use natural speech with a computer. Whether it was called "natural speech recognition" or "artificial intelligence," such technology promised to open a new horizon of possibilities. And if any company seemed likely to break this technical barrier, it was InterVoice-Brite; since it first incorporated speech recognition into a 1986 product, InterVoice had been a leader in the field.

This was a position it planned to jealously defend. Even while it was preparing for the Brite acquisition, InterVoice had continued to develop cutting-edge speech applications. SpeechAccess, its family of advanced speech recognition products that used technology from Speechworks International, debuted in early 1999 and was quickly upgraded to operate in a Windows NT environment.[9]

At the same time, InterVoice announced an original equipment manufacturing (OEM) agreement with Nuance Communications, a premier

The InVision graphical interface. InVision, InterVoice-Brite's development tool, was the industry's leading easy-to-use speech recognition script program.

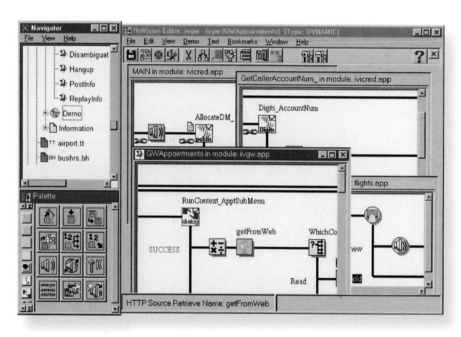

supplier of natural-language speech recognition, to integrate Nuance's software into the InVision script development program as well as Speechworks. The resulting product, InVision SpeechWizard, enabled application developers to easily design and implement speech recognition call flow scripts. For the first time, IVR application developers could design call flow scripts without complex programming.[10]

SpeechAccess quickly established itself as the industry's leading automated speech system. With it, engineers could add a natural-speech interface to automated call processing systems for a wide variety of applications, including car and hotel rentals, airline tickets, stock transactions, banking, and even prescription refills.

"Speech recognition has evolved from a novelty to a real-world technology that companies are using to improve their bottom lines," said Ron Owens, senior manager of InterVoice-Brite's Advanced Speech Development team. "InterVoice and Speechworks have been instrumental in making speech recognition commercially viable on a highly reliable and expandable platform that customers can configure to suit their needs."[11]

As Speechworks CEO Stuart Patterson observed, SpeechAccess had numerous uses, including direct application in the finance business.

"The fastest-moving part of the brokerage industry is those firms that have adapted to the Web," Patterson said. "Our system, through natural language processing, allows a user to speak naturally, as there are over thirty thousand different combinations of words to indicate any particular stock or exchange."[12]

By 2002, the market for speech recognition technology was predicted to balloon to $1.1 billion, or almost tenfold in three years.[13] InterVoice-Brite stood to reap great rewards. Not only did it have the industry's best script development tool and an established proprietary hardware platform; it had also partnered with the two leading speech technology companies.

Customers Sign On

The market responded. Businesses ranging from airlines to banks to insurance companies began to switch from Touch-Tone to directed dialogue speech with the widespread expectation that within two years they would switch again to natural-speech-recognition engines.

"Natural speech recognition really changes the paradigm for the customer by making the interaction with the computer humanlike," said Walt Mirkowicz, vice president of Platform Product Units. "People don't want to follow an algorithm—step one, two, three—to get their answer. They don't have enough patience to stay within its parameters. They want to get to the point and address their issue immediately."[14]

In May 2000, InterVoice-Brite announced the addition of name recognition and multilingual capabilities. Amazingly, the company had also developed a database that could recognize more than 80 percent of the first and last names in the United States and simultaneously support two or more languages.[15]

As corporations implemented systems, consumer acceptance surged rapidly. In October 2000, a consumer survey conducted by Evans Research showed that speech recognition had become the preferred method for accessing information and services via the telephone. More than 80 percent of consumers preferred speech recognition systems to Touch-Tone, Internet, or even speaking with live agents and operators. Satisfaction was even higher among wireless users.[16]

In response, InterVoice-Brite continued to add features to SpeechAccess. Before long, the product would offer a next-generation text-to-speech (TTS) engine from Speechworks. The Speechify TTS engine converted text into natural-sounding male and female speech, making the system's vocabulary virtually unlimited. It allowed callers to hear text-based information—such as e-mail or Web content—using any telephone.[17]

XML

At the same time it was developing Speech-Access, InterVoice-Brite announced it was extending the capabilities of its renowned OneVoice voice and call automation platform to support XML (eXtensible markup language) as a standard transaction connectivity option. At the time, XML was fast becoming the new standard in data communication.[18] Voice XML (VXML) is comparable to HTML (hypertext markup language): Whereas HTML refers

Integrated Speech Recognition Improves Overall Security

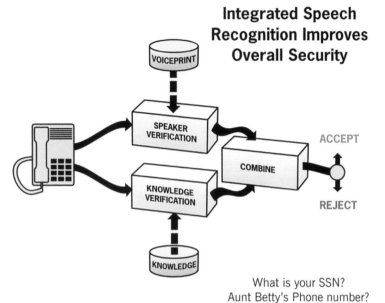

What is your SSN?
Aunt Betty's Phone number?

Above: Natural speech recognition continued to advance in the early years of the millennium. This graphic illustrates IVR speech security, which was especially important for m-commerce (mobile commerce) applications.

Right: Skip Cave, pictured in 2002, has been a part of InterVoice since its inception. He had worked with founder Dan Hammond on the first voice board two decades before.

Below: Craig Evans, pictured in 2002, joined Intervoice in the 1980s and is currently the director of Premium Accounts for the enterprise business.

years before we see widespread adoption, but it is now clear that voice is a necessary component in any e-commerce strategy."[20]

By standardizing Web-based voice communication, some analysts predicted that VXML would do for the telecommunications community what cable television had done for communications providers. According to Terry Gold, CEO of Gold Systems, an independent provider of IVR and wireless Web systems for *Fortune*-100 businesses, "Phone access to the Web is the next hot market, and by adopting the VoiceXML specification as a standard, companies can develop and deploy voice-to-Web applications quicker and more cost effectively."[21]

For clients using InterVoice-Brite systems, VXML was able to standardize data communication across a range of applications, including voice automation and Web-based voice portals. These voice portals, which allowed callers to dial into databases and receive news, sports, financial data, and other information, were steadily growing in popularity.

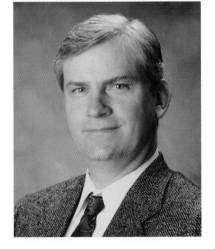

"You call a number and it will answer, 'Hello, this is Tell Me,'" said InterVoice-Brite engineer Skip Cave. "You say 'sports, basketball, Mavericks,' and it will start reading the Mavericks score to you. Portals are becoming a hot deal, and some dot.com companies have started as portal companies. We're scratching our heads, saying, 'You know, we've been doing exactly that for many years.'"[22]

to Web pages, VXML refers to how information is presented for voice.

"Traditionally, various IVR vendors have all really invented their own language that describes the applications," said Craig Evans, director of Premium Accounts for InterVoice-Brite Enterprise Solutions Division. "VXML is an attempt to standardize that."[19]

"I believe VXML is an amazing technology that will certainly find a home in e-commerce," agreed voice- and data-communications industry analyst Brian Strachman. "It will be several

VXML was also an important element in InterVoice-Brite's growing ASP market. For example, a large financial institution that relied on multiple platforms could use an InterVoice-Brite–managed VXML system to access customer information in a common database, reducing the bank's overhead and enhancing the value of its existing infrastructure.

The power of XML was especially appealing to telecommunications companies. By 2001, despite the downturn, the next generation of technology began to appear on the market. These new technologies, often referred to as third generation (3G), were wireless, Internet-enabled, and cross-functional. They offered voice, data, limited video capabilities, and Internet access from anywhere.

Naturally, InterVoice-Brite sought to convert these devices to voice—even before they had achieved deep market penetration. It was a logical step since many wireless devices relied on tedious and sometimes tiny keyboards or mousepads. InterVoice-Brite envisioned a day in the near future when wireless and hand-held devices would be fully voice activated and connected to voice networks and databases. It wasn't long before VXML was added to OneVoice.[23]

"A lot of things people are used to doing on their computers, they will someday be able to do through their telephone handsets," commented Abhay Sawant, InterVoice-Brite head of unified messaging. "We can talk to our PCs; we should be able to talk to our handsets as well."[24]

As it worked toward the next generation of speech products, InterVoice-Brite continued to refine its business and pay down debt. In February the company sold a block of shares in Speechworks International that it had acquired several years before in conjunction with a supplier agreement. This sale brought in approximately $21.4 million, which InterVoice-Brite used pay down its debt.[25] By February 2001, it owed only $46.1 million from the acquisition of Brite Voice.[26]

Omvia

In early 2001, InterVoice-Brite's Network Solutions Division announced a major technological advance known as Omvia, which was designed principally for the telecommunications market. The Omvia suite of products included communications portals, messaging, unified communications, secure m-commerce services, and prepaid and postpaid calling. It represented more than thirty years of combined InterVoice and Brite Systems development experience, as well as input from other major communi-

cations and e-business leaders through key alliances. By March, Omvia had been introduced worldwide.

"Our major effort over this last year has been to make value-added services more customer oriented," said Ray Naeini, president of Network Solutions.

Omvia is a family of operations that will provide easy-to-use services that subscribers and consumers can get in addition to basic voice and data services. It is unified communication, such as accessing your voice message, e-mail, and fax. It pretty much revolutionizes the way we communicate and do business. . . . We are delivering new economy promises based on the old economy strength that we have.[27]

Omvia's functionality was almost limitless. The name Omvia, in fact, stood for "omni," or "universally," and "via," or "through," suggesting that customers could get everything they needed through the product. For example, businesspeople could pick up any type of message (e-mail, fax, voice mail) from any phone and dictate e-mail replies; grandparents could receive e-mail from their grandchildren and reply simply by talking to the household telephone; and students could receive any information from any Web site, at home, without a PC.[28] Omvia technology adapted itself to the situation, making communications easy, seamless, and voice activated.

Omvia enriched the subscriber's experience while also improving a carrier's competitive position. For carriers that wanted to increase traffic on an existing network or recoup the cost of new technologies, Omvia could support virtually any services strategy at any phase of network migration.[29] Omvia was also offered through the Communication Application Service Provider (CASP) Group so that if companies didn't want to purchase the technology outright, they could outsource the entire function to InterVoice-Brite.

Three months after the introduction of Omvia, InterVoice-Brite Network Solutions announced it had received a $6.5 million order from a major distributor to supply Omvia to an overseas cellular provider.[30] By the end of the year, InterVoice-Brite announced that VXML had been incorporated into Omvia.[31]

As it developed and was deployed, one of the critical advantages of Omvia quickly became apparent. It wasn't simply a labor-saving device; it represented a competitive advantage to telecommunications companies.

"The telephone company has figured out that it is going to be more expensive and tougher to lure new customers," said Network Solutions Division Executive Vice President Scotty Walsh. "So it has to figure out how to get more revenue from the same customers. How do you do that? Well, you offer them new products and services that they can't get from somewhere else."[32]

Eventually, Walsh predicted, telecommunications providers would offer a kind of advanced voice portal using Omvia. Customers would be able to call a provider and be greeted by name by a computer. They could then navigate through their billing, calling plans, options, and other services easily and quickly. When combined with unified messaging and natural language recognition, this kind of service seemed almost futuristic—but it wasn't really that far off.

Wireless and Prepaid Take Off

When this future arrived, it would likely not be connected to only a landline phone. By May 2000, the number of mobile subscribers worldwide was already twice the number of Internet users (428 million to 241 million), according to the ARC Group—and the addition of 3G mobile data capabilities was expected to fuel further wireless-market growth. The ARC Group predicted 800 million wireless data access terminals in use within three years.[33]

This move toward wireless added another range of possibilities, especially with the Internet. By 2005 an estimated 1.5 billion people would have access to the Internet, and more would access the Internet from a wireless device than from a PC.[34] InterVoice-Brite's strategy was driven by the explosive growth anticipated in the wireless, Internet, and speech technology markets.[35] In late 2001, the company announced a strategic alliance with 724 solutions to develop a product that would make the mobile Internet viable.[36]

Up until this point, the wireless Internet had been an effective medium for receiving information, but it remained limited by the number of "clicks and scrolls" needed to request the information. Speech recognition could overcome this obstacle by allowing callers to speak their requests as they navigated through the Internet. This feature would be offered in addition to unified messaging, voice service, paging, e-mail, shopping, and even scheduling programs like personal digital assistants (PDAs).

"The wireless phone may become a PDA, a GPS terminal, and an e-commerce wireless credit card," said CEO David Brandenburg. "When people are on a wireless phone, most of the time they are in a position where they can't use a keyboard, so they need speech recognition technology on the other end so they can get information. Most of our customers will be enhancing their systems with speech recognition or speech user interface."[37]

The rise of wireless technology in the United States coincided with a boom in prepaid phone plans. For several years, prepaid calling had experienced greater success in Europe and the developing world than in the United States. At least in the developing world, the reason was fairly simple: It was cheaper and easier to build wireless infrastructure.

"In places like Africa and Latin America, instead of developing landlines like we did and then moving to wireless, they went first to wireless," Brandenburg said. "Also, wireless is a less-expensive infrastructure."[38]

Prepaid was popular in developing countries that lacked the sophisticated lending institutions found in the United States and Europe. However, once Americans accepted the idea of prepaid service, they did it with fervor. The sale of phone cards in the United States grew from $12 million in 1992 to $4.17 billion in 1999, according to the Telecommunications Industry Association.

InterVoice-Brite recognized that another new market was opening. Prepaid services often relied on IVR to reload a prepaid calling card by applying a charge to a credit card account.[39]

M-commerce also promised to expand in the future as people began turning to their wireless devices for shopping and other transactions. InterVoice-Brite launched programs to leverage its existing prepaid wireless platform to develop m-commerce capabilities.[40]

The InterVoice-Brite world headquarters, Dallas. From this campus, the company directed operations throughout a global network of offices and suppliers. Brite's senior employees relocated to Texas after the acquisition.

A Global Competitor

The trend toward globalization continued as InterVoice-Brite's many competitors angled for their own share of the market. In the IVR market, Intervoice-Brite was the only company with a market share that exceeded 10 percent. It had a huge installed base of systems, including about twenty thousand systems shipped to customers in more than seventy-four countries.[41] Its principle competitors included Avaya and Nortel Networks. In the ASP business, InterVoice had little competition, and in the telecommunications network systems, it competed against Comverse Technology.[42]

International customers were attracted to InterVoice-Brite products for a number of reasons, including the ease with which buyers could customize applications in foreign languages; the ability of the company's systems to support multiple languages concurrently, to interact with rotary phones, and to support voice recognition when Touch-Tone phones were unavailable; and the company's efforts in obtaining the required approvals for connectivity to the telephone networks in numerous international markets.[43]

The company's international sales mushroomed 434 percent in 2000 because of the acquisition of Brite.[44] InterVoice-Brite now maintained offices in the United Kingdom, the Netherlands, Switzerland, Germany, Italy, Dubai, and South Africa. Although a subsidiary was located in Brazil, the majority of

sales to Latin America were conducted through Dallas offices. InterVoice-Brite also maintained small offices in Montreal, Toronto, and Vancouver.

Overseas sales were aided by deregulation. In the late 1990s, the European Union deregulated its telecommunications market, and around the same time a wave of market liberalization swept through the technology-thirsty economies of Japan, Singapore, and elsewhere. In Asia, perhaps more than anywhere else, wireless technology was the communication method of choice. The Asia Pacific region constituted about half of the world's population and had the world's largest base of wireless subscribers.

The long-term opportunity in Asia was actually enhanced by the so-called Asian flu, a late-1990s economic crisis that swept the rapidly developing economies of Indonesia, Thailand, Singapore, Malaysia, Taiwan, and others. In response to tight budgets and hard-to-get credit, Asian corporations sought cost-effective solutions, including an increased reliance on IVR and managed services.[45]

Japan, too, represented a huge market. As the world's second-largest economy, Japan's telephony market was more developed than that of the United States, with 14 percent more mobile penetration—about 66.8 million subscribers.[46] Automation was widespread in Japan because of high labor costs, and speech-enabled systems were rapidly gaining acceptance because of foreign competition in the banking, Internet, and telecom markets.[47]

In early 2001, to strengthen its existing office in Singapore and increase coverage in the Asia Pacific region, InterVoice-Brite opened an office in Tokyo.[48] That year, the company offered enterprise products outside the United States through a global sales force of fifteen and a network of more than forty-five distributors. Its international network products were sold by a separate international sales force of approximately forty.[49]

The Business Develops

Within its established global and technological framework, InterVoice-Brite had settled into a recognizable form by 2002. The Network Solutions Division provided telco carriers and Internet service providers with value-added communication and e-business services and software under the

Omvia and BriteStar product names. It represented a little more than half of sales. Enterprise Solutions delivered speech and call-automation systems to a broad range of customers worldwide.[50]

Both divisions shared some core technologies, such as digital signal processor (DSP) technology, advanced speech recognition capabilities, application development tools, and the CASP infrastructure. They also borrowed technology from each other. Network Solutions, for example, borrowed the InVision development tool, while Enterprise Solutions integrated some of Network Solutions' large-network technology.

With its complete range of offerings, InterVoice-Brite was the only company in the world that could boast seventeen years of experience in the voice industry.[51]

In early 2001, the company announced that it was working with one of the world's foremost banking institutions to provide a voice-driven application that would enable the bank's customers in Europe to speak naturally to an automated telephone system.[52] Though Europe had been quick to embrace new communications technologies, speech recognition applications were not yet used extensively by banks in many European countries.

"Our extensive experience with speech applications and with automating transactions for financial institutions gave us the edge over other solutions vendors," said Bob Ritchey, president of Enterprise Solutions. "We believe many more opportunities are forthcoming as other European banks recognize the potential cost savings and increased customer satisfaction offered by automated speech solutions."[53]

Omvia continued to gain in popularity around the globe. Throughout the year, orders were

received from customers in Germany, central Europe, India, and Turkey. In Turkey, InterVoice-Brite became the power behind Turkey's first speech recognition service when Global Securities, Turkey's leading independent financial house, launched that country's first speech-enabled call automation system.[54]

Then in late 2001, InterVoice-Brite announced that Omvia had received Ericsson certification. Under the certification, InterVoice-Brite's unified messaging and voicemail/faxmail communications platform was fully integrated into Ericsson's existing network equipment.[55]

The CASP group continued to be a driving force in InterVoice-Brite's future strategy.[56] Through the CASP group, a telecommunications provider could straddle all the various emerging networks without a huge capital investment. This ability represented a real competitive advantage in the form of better service. With four accredited network operations centers (in Cambridge and Manchester, England, and Orlando and Wichita in the United States), InterVoice-Brite could markets its CASP model to telco carriers and traditional IVR customers.

"We are probably the largest ASP out there, and we've had very good experience in terms of how we manage the capital, manage the finances, and manage the outsourcing," said Ray Naeini, president of the Network Solutions Division. "The ASP is a very good model."[57]

In June 2001, Network Solutions announced an eighteen-

The NSP-5000. By 2002, the issue of switching existing Brite customers to InterVoice hardware platforms had faded into the background.

month extension of its contract with BT/Cellnet to provide prepaid mobile phone service for its United Kingdom customers.[58] BT/Cellnet, part of British Telecom, had approximately 10.5 million customers using its voice services, including more than one million customers with mobile Internet-enabled phones. The cumulative value of the contract extension was approximately $16.6 million.

"The cost and risk-sharing benefits associated with our unique and proven ASP model will allow forward-thinking operators [like BT/Cellnet] to continue upgrading their networks with enhanced services as they employ 3G technologies," remarked Naeini.[59]

The Network Solutions Division expanded further in October 2001, when it introduced Omvia Professional Services, which provided a number of flexible service options including consulting and business services, Omvia product customization and integration of third-party products, Omvia Care, technical support, monitoring and surveillance, and disaster recovery services.[60]

The Customer Challenge

InterVoice-Brite's products were designed with customers in mind—whether InterVoice-Brite's immediate customers or the ultimate end users of the technology. The company boasted that its IVR products could save as much as $1 per phone call, which, when multiplied by millions of calls at a large corporation, represented substantial savings. And yet these savings didn't accrue at the expense of end users. Just the opposite.

Customers were savvier and more empowered than ever before. In the telecommunications industry, agents were expected to service customers via telephone, fax, e-mail, and the Internet.[61] In the banking industry, financial institutions raced to offer as many contact points as possible, from automated teller machines to voice-enabled databases. At the same time, the banking industry was undergoing recurring waves of consolidation, with sometimes mixed results.

"Some of the larger bank customers have their own consolidation issues," Rob-Roy Graham, CFO, said. "We've been finding that as a response to less-than-expected earnings, many of our banking customers are now very, very receptive to ASP

services because they can keep on the leading edge of applications and customer service without having to make a large, up-front capital investment."[62]

As new information and choices flooded the economy, consumers became more demanding. They could scour the Internet for the best deal. They could buy goods and services on-line, by phone, or in person. If a business wasn't successful in earning a customer's loyalty, that person was likely to go elsewhere.[63] The buzzword for this all-important art of keeping customers happy is customer relationship management (CRM). The CRM market included any device or technology that allowed a company to stay close to its customer base and somehow make customers' lives easier. Analysts projected that the CRM market would reach $4.45 billion in 2001.[64]

"In the digital age, customers expect better, faster and friendlier service and become impatient if it is absent," wrote Andrew Fisher in *Financial Times Limited*. "As mobile commerce develops, people will become even more demanding."[65]

InterVoice-Brite, whose products both saved money and earned revenue, was firmly entrenched in the CRM market. The company's solutions were designed specifically to put its customers at the leading edge of the emerging mobile society with a mind-boggling array of services.

"The market is exciting again," said InterVoice-Brite board member George Platt Sr. "With true speech being added to the technology, the amount of opportunity, especially in Third World countries, has increased substantially."[66]

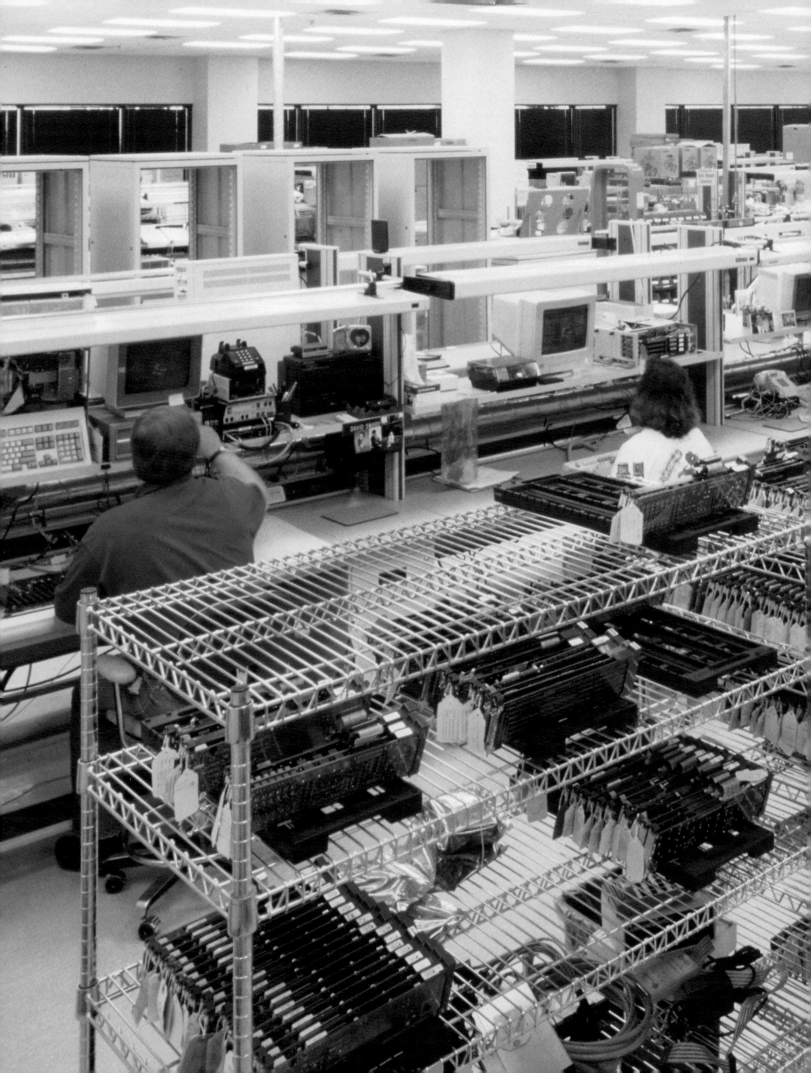

By this time, InterVoice-Brite had accomplished an incredible feat. It had grown exponentially in one of the world's most competitive businesses. In just two decades, the company had evolved into a global organization that offered comprehensive call automation solutions spanning enterprise and telecommunications markets.

This growth in revenue, geographical reach, and technological expertise represented the maturation of a true start-up. When it was founded, InterVoice was powered by a small group of engineers and salesmen driven by the vision of the troika of Dan Hammond, Mike Tessarowicz, and Al Fleener. At its founding, the company was product driven, moving steadily into deeper waters by incorporating the newest technology into voice-activated products. Unlike most of its competitors, InterVoice-Brite was both a hardware and a software company—a full-service IVR shop. InterVoice-Brite maintained that legacy as it passed the $300 million mark in revenue.

Always technically savvy, much of InterVoice-Brite's development would come on the sales side, complements of David Brandenburg. From his vantage point, Brandenburg frequently pushed InterVoice-Brite to develop its sales capacity.

Although the industry and the general economy were slumping, and challenges remained for the network business, InterVoice-Brite had survived and prospered in one of the world's toughest markets. Nevertheless, ominous signs outside the company, including the continued weakness in the telecommunications industry and a general recession that began in March 2001, gave company leaders pause.

September 11, 2001

Throughout 2001, Brandenburg moved to shield InterVoice-Brite from the deleterious effects of the slowing economy. Although painful, this strategy worked. Then late in the year, an international tragedy changed everything. On September

Opposite: Employees in InterVoice-Brite's fabrication operation. The company led its industry in manufacturing its own products, including the basic voice boards.

11, 2001, terrorists attacked the World Trade Center and the Pentagon with three hijacked passenger airliners. A fourth crashed in rural Pennsylvania. All told, more than 3,000 people died as a result of the attacks, and the United States economy was hobbled by the acts.

InterVoice-Brite, like many companies, joined a spontaneous national outpouring of grief and patriotism. Employees throughout InterVoice-Brite donated money to the victims' families. Their donations were matched by the Brandenburg Life Foundation and sent on to the stricken cities. InterVoice-Brite next established a relief fund for the victims and families in New York City and Washington, D.C. Employees were encouraged to contribute to this fund, and final donations were collected just a few weeks following the catastrophic events. The company collected almost $44,000 and donated the majority of the sum to the Twin Towers Fund, established by former New York Mayor Rudolph Giuliani to support the families of uniformed service heroes affected by the disaster.

Shortly after the attacks, the economic effects began to set in. "Everything just stopped," remembered CEO David Brandenburg. "After that, things just did not quite regain the momentum they had beforehand."

In the months afterward, the nation was beset by a series of high-profile layoffs as the airline, high technology, and telecommunications industries hemorrhaged skilled workers. According to InterVoice-Brite Vice President of Human Resources Don Brown, the "floodgates really opened up."

Naturally, InterVoice-Brite was dramatically affected and saw its already weakened business further erode. In early 2002, David Brandenburg chose to take further action. He announced a major reorganization of InterVoice-Brite's business. This time, the Wichita office was to be closed and its Network Solutions operations moved to Dallas. Similarly, the Jacksonville office would be relocated to Orlando, run by Mac Hammond, the last of the Hammond brothers to join InterVoice-Brite. Finally, Brandenburg announced that 102 employees in the United States and 23 overseas would be laid off and some new marketing and sales positions added.

"While job losses will unfortunately be associated with these actions, we will also be creating

![iVB Enterprise Solutions — A Division of InterVoice-Brite, Inc.]

additional new jobs, many of which will be in our upgraded sales and marketing efforts," Brandenburg wrote to his employees. "In this regard, we have previously stated our intention to increase sales and marketing staff by 50 percent, with an emphasis on engaging experienced personnel who had the ability and contacts to work with present and potential customers at a higher organizational level."

Within the divisions, leadership was confident during the reorganization. In the Enterprise Solutions Division, President Bob Ritchey, who had recently joined the company from Honeywell, announced, "We will restructure ourselves to be a more focused and flatter organization, allowing all departments to work closely with senior management." The new organization allowed the Enter-

prise Division to concentrate more keenly on VXML, wireless data, and Web-based technology.

Rather than representing a statement on InterVoice-Brite's overall business or strategy, the reorganization was more correctly seen as yet another refinement in the company's continuing quest to best approach two very different markets that often used the same technology. In fact, as Brandenburg pointed out, InterVoice-Brite continued to add sales and marketing employees at the same time that other companies were downsizing their sales function.

Much of this strategy had to do with focus. Unlike many companies, InterVoice-Brite remained true to the vision of its founders. When they created the first IVR system to run on a PC, they had correctly discerned the shape of the future: One day, voice capability would be essential because people are vocal creatures.

Since that seminal moment, InterVoice-Brite assembled the technology and mustered the willpower to reach the day when human and machine could seamlessly and easily communicate. A team of experienced industry veterans, led by CEO David Brandenburg, had coalesced to guide the company toward this day.

The Telecom Meltdown

Unfortunately, although InterVoice-Brite was rapidly changing to meet its markets, the industry would change even faster. After the terrorist attacks, the U.S. economy would begin limping out of its recession by early 2002. But not every segment could make that claim, especially companies that relied on business-to-business sales. In particular, the telecommunications sector continued its downward spiral. As a rule, the big players were overinvested in fiber-optic technology, and the competition from wireless technology was wreaking havoc in long-distance pricing. Even this plight might not have been catastrophic, however,

Bob Ritchey, then president of the Enterprise Solutions Division of InterVoice. The Enterprise Solutions Division sold speech and IVR systems to banks and other large entities.

except for a string of events that no one could have foreseen during the boom of the mid-1990s.

Oddly enough, the debacle began with an oil-trading company called Enron. At one time a stodgy utility, Enron had reshaped the energy business in the mid-1990s by pioneering the on-line energy market. In early 2002, however, Enron made a surprise announcement: It would have to soon restate earnings because it had overstated them by hundreds of millions of dollars.

Although this admission seemed remarkable enough, it was nothing compared with the string of revelations that followed. Within a few short months, a disgusted public absorbed a tale of unethical and disastrous accounting schemes set up by Enron to deliberately falsify its earnings, thus propping up the stock price while company executives bailed out of their positions. Less than six months after its first announcement, Enron declared bankruptcy in the largest bankruptcy case in American history. Tens of thousands of investors lost their investment.

Had this been an isolated incident, maybe the damage to the telecom sector would have stopped. But the Enron debacle was only the beginning. Over the next months, company after company was forced to reveal similar accounting scandals. In their particulars, these cases were all different. But when added together, it seemed that all of corporate America was padding the numbers one way or another.

Unfortunately for companies like InterVoice-Brite, whose numbers were never questioned, the telecommunications sector was hit especially hard by accounting scandals. Only a few months after Enron, telecommunications giant WorldCom—owner of the famous MCI brand—revealed its own accounting irregularities and was soon teetering on the edge of bankruptcy. It joined a list of troubled telecommunications companies that included Global Crossing, Qwest, Adelphia, and Excel.

Finally, the stock market could withstand no more. Over the summer of 2002, the Dow Jones Industrial Average lost about 30 percent of its value, falling from around 11,000 to less than 8,000. The telecommunications industry, already in a slump and beset by the high-profile accounting scandals, tanked. InterVoice-Brite, roughly half of which was devoted to telecommunications network sales through the former Brite, was blindsided. At one point in July 2002, its stock traded for less than a dollar a share. And although sales in the first quarter represented a quarter-over-quarter gain and an increase in backlog, they came to only around $38 million. At that rate, InterVoice-Brite could expect sales of $150 million, down from a high of almost $300 million.

In response, InterVoice-Brite's leaders began crafting a way to overcome the toughest industry conditions in memory.

Intervoice CEO David Brandenburg, a marathon runner, led the company through the tumultuous early twenty-first century.

CHAPTER NINE

TWO DECADES AND BEYOND

2002–2003

[January–March 2002] has been a transition quarter. We focused on the enterprise business. In the next couple quarters, we're going to focus on the network business. If everything falls right, we should see a much better profit picture coming in.

—Bob Ritchey, 2002

IT WOULDN'T TAKE LONG FOR InterVoice-Brite to react to the difficult business conditions. In mid-2002, Ray Naeini, president of the hobbled Network Division, left the company. Shortly afterward, CEO David Brandenburg set off to talk with employees in Orlando, Florida; Manchester, England; Dubai, United Arab Emirates; and Dallas, Texas.

"I had the opportunity not only to talk to my senior guys, but to talk to everybody and get their input on what they see out there from a customer perspective," Brandenburg said. "I came back and shared their perspectives with Bob Ritchey, and Bob went to his staff and put all that together. It didn't all come from the top down."[1]

In summer 2002, Brandenburg announced that InterVoice-Brite would take the next natural step in its evolution. In the coming months, the Network Solutions Division would be combined with the Enterprise Division, except in the critical areas of product marketing and product management. Everything else, including research and development, customer support, and special services, would be combined.

This reorganization, said Brandenburg, not only made the most sense for InterVoice-Brite's current size; it also yielded the best of both worlds by maintaining product differentiation and eliminating the overlapping layers within the two-division structure.

Naturally, this move would require another downsizing, the fourth in six months. This subject, Brandenburg knew, would have to be broached very carefully with employees, who had witnessed several restructurings and were naturally nervous.

"What we decided to do was be very, very open," Brandenburg said.

Normally in these situations your senior people get together, and they decide what's going to happen. You really don't tell the whole employee base about it until the day it happens. What we decided to do was to tell people in advance what we were going to do.[2]

In early summer 2002, the executive team of InterVoice-Brite met with teams of employees and managers. Rob-Roy Graham, CFO, delivered a presentation to employees all over the world, together with the rest of the senior management team. Graham's detailed analysis showed what the company expected from the future. While it was clear that there would be fewer people, these

---

Bob Ritchey, an industry veteran, was promoted to president in 2002 as the company reorganized its operating units back into a single division.

presentations also helped build a sense of hope and faith within the company.

Intervoice: A Name Change

Other steps were also taken. As InterVoice-Brite prepared to morph into a single division, David Brandenburg requested a shareholder vote to change the name of the company from InterVoice-Brite to Intervoice. There was a good reason for this. The name InterVoice-Brite was not a particularly memorable or marketable name. Intervoice, however, still had all the panache it had always carried. The name change was approved at the annual shareholders' meeting in August 2002. Henceforth the company was known only as Intervoice.

Aligned as a single brand, the new name reflected the full integration of products, services, operations, and personnel between the former InterVoice and Brite companies. The company began working to establish a new market image consistent with the converging marketplace and the new global customer requirements.

"These are things that will be good in the long term," said Brandenburg, "that we're being forced to do a little earlier by the market."[3]

Around the same time, Bob Ritchey, president of the Enterprise Solutions Division, was named president of the company. Before joining Intervoice-Brite in December 2000, Ritchey had been with Honeywell's Home Business Controls Division. Before that, he had gained telecommunications experience at Nortel, where he managed their messaging and Interactive Voice Response product lines.

The Line of Business (LOB) structure was the most significant part of the reorganization. In order to create a leaner yet functionally stronger skills-based organization, LOB enabled Intervoice to focus on its defined markets and products. The organizational alignment removed all walls and barriers, allowing the company the operate as a unified business.

Finally, to help fund its current operations, Intervoice secured a $10 million credit line to restructure its debt load. The deal stirred up some controversy among the regular financial press. Under the terms of the placement, Intervoice issued convertible notes worth $10 million. When the notes came due, in about September, Intervoice owed about $1 million a month in cash. If it couldn't pay, it had the option of issuing new stock to pay the debt.

Intervoice, however, was confident that it would be able to repay the loan with cash on hand. As company officers pointed out, the underlying market dynamics of the enterprise division were fundamentally sound, and there was still network market opportunity overseas. This enterprise portion had been affected, but only mildly compared to

1983: ITA founders Dan Hammond and Mike Tessarowicz make their first sale.

1989: InterVoice moves into new corporate headquarters on Waterview Parkway in Dallas.

1991: InterVoice makes a daunting switch to the OS/2 operating system and opens a Paris office.

1985: The company's name is changed to InterVoice, and it goes public.

1990: David Brandenburg joins the company as COO.

the network division. Based on these factors and Intervoice's effort to cut costs, Graham was able to confidently predict that the company would meet its loan obligations.

In fact, the loan was paid off by fall 2002 and was replaced by a new line of more conventional financing.

An Open Standard

In a short-term business sense, 2001 and 2002 were difficult times. Intervoice struggled to deal with one blow after another to its industry and was forced to downsize and reorganize several times to meet the changing circumstances. Moreover, the expected turnaround took longer than most industry observers had predicted.

Yet by 2002, the signs of recovery were already there. Intervoice had restructured its debt, and positive news once again flowed from the company's headquarters in Dallas. In October 2002, Intervoice announced an alliance with Microsoft to create open, standards-based speech solutions for Web designers. Under the terms of the three-year alliance, the two companies would jointly develop and market a speech-based platform for MS.NET. This speech platform would be based on Speech Application Language Tags (SALT), an open-standard platform that made large-scale enterprise speech applications significantly easier to create.

It was a good move for both companies. Microsoft gained access to Intervoice's proven expertise in speech solutions development and its giant pool of customers. In return, Intervoice gained access to Microsoft's unmatched development and marketing, and the software giant would promote Intervoice to its enterprise customers as a "leader in deploying speech solutions on the MS.NET speech platform."[4]

In order to gain market leadership in SALT-based development tools and applications, in October 2002 Bob Ritchey appointed John Donaldson to assume overall responsibility for the Microsoft relationship and for product strategy related to SALT-based initiatives.

"An alliance with Microsoft is important to the long-term Intervoice strategy of migration to an open-systems model," said Donaldson, Intervoice's vice president of strategic product development. "The alliance with Microsoft will also help Intervoice achieve its goal of helping customers to leverage their investment in existing IT infrastructure by providing the most flexible and efficient technologies possible."[5]

Although the alliance had not reflected on Intervoice's bottom line, it was hailed as a seminal moment in the industry. "This alliance signals a paradigm shift from proprietary systems to Web-based speech solutions that are based on open standards," said Brian Strachman, an analyst with

1993: InterVoice breaks ground on the Carter Building, a new corporate headquarters.

1999: InterVoice acquires Brite Voice Systems, of Orlando, Florida, and doubles in size.

1995: InterVoice attains ISO 9001 certification.

2002: InterVoice-Brite changes its name to Intervoice. The company announces a software development alliance with Microsoft.

In-Stat/MDR. "Microsoft's speech technologies are making it faster and easier than ever before for developers and enterprises to extend their Web investments with speech."[6]

The SALT strategy dovetailed with Intervoice's focus on VXML, another open-standard application tool. Intervoice figured that one or the other would eventually evolve as the industry standard, and the company planned to be current when that happened. In an effort to elaborate on the alliance, Intervoice answered the questions within a positioning document: "Why is Intervoice supporting SALT? What about the investment Intervoice has in VXML?"

Diana and David Brandenburg. In 2002, Brandenburg studied the problems facing Intervoice and charted a course into the future, including reorganizing and renaming the company.

Intervoice continues to support VXML. Yet in order to provide more choices to our customers, the Intervoice strategy is to further develop the applications and tools space and adopt MS.NET architecture and platforms like ASP.NET and Visual Studio.NET. This relationship furthers that goal by enabling Intervoice to produce SALT-based speech applications on what Microsoft and Intervoice believe will become the standard industry speech platform (MS.NET Speech).[7]

In the meantime, the company would also continue to support its customers with proprietary products, pledging to "work with them to migrate to a more flexible, economical, extensible, open, standards-based solution."[8]

With excitement and momentum once again building behind the company, a clearer picture began to emerge about what had really happened over the previous two years. And despite the painful measures, it was a positive story. Intervoice had held through a wrenching industry-wide correction and recession, a time when business-to-business spending all but vanished. Intervoice's senior leadership had very little doubt that the company was on the right track. Its technology, especially its still-developing VXML and SALT products, was becoming increasingly accepted in a steadily

expanding world of communications options. If it took some time for the technologies to standardize and the markets to shake out—and that shakeout hit Intervoice's bottom line—that was how free markets operated.

"By and large, I think the employee base takes it as very positive," said Mike Polcyn, an Intervoice veteran who was promoted to senior vice president, research and development, as part of the reorganization.

We're moving into a fourth round with this company. First there was the true entrepreneurial startup. Then David Brandenburg came in, professionalizing the business. The third was the growth and the acquisition of Brite. And the fourth is moving into yet another round of professionalizing the organization, moving toward a sustainable business model where we're bringing in some high-powered professional managers like Bob Ritchey and moving toward a strategy and planning model.[9]

Throughout its twenty years, Intervoice remained a technology leader and market innovator ready to seize on the various opportunities in its market. In fact, said Bob Ritchey, Intervoice might soon find a new market for messaging products because many of the existing systems, produced by Lucent, were growing old and had no product support. This created an opportunity for Intervoice to replace them. Similarly, the voice portal business and the traditional IVR business continued to show promise.

"This has been a transition quarter," Ritchey said in the middle of 2002. "We focused on the enterprise business. In the next couple quarters, we're going to focus on the network business. If everything falls right, we should see a much better profit picture coming in."[10]

He was right. By the end of 2002, Intervoice was on solid footing with new customers, new partnerships, improved morale and revenue, and even a new branding strategy. New customers included Safaricom, Michigan Department of Treasury, Neiman Marcus, Centrelink, SunTrust, AdvancePCS, and America First Credit Union. In the December 2002 employee newsletter, company President Bob Ritchey wrote, "2002 has definitely been an eventful year for all of us."

Despite a challenging economic climate and an industry that's in constant change, Intervoice continues to aggressively embrace new technology

and emerging partners to provide the best solutions for our customers.[11]

Ritchey pointed out some positive developments from the year past, including the company's migration to open systems development with SALT and VXML, its role in making speech-activated applications mainstream, and its global impact on the mobile communications industry. "There are a lot of good things we've done in the last six months," he said in early 2003. "We had a good third quarter, we announced an alliance with Microsoft, and we've stabilized the organization."[12]

The stabilization included Intervoice's products. The Omvia brand, which had begun development as a network product, was expanded to

Inset: In late 2002, John Donaldson assumed overall responsibility for Intervoice's relationship with Microsoft. The companies were jointly developing voice products for MS.NET.

Below: Even as the rest of the economy grudgingly recovered in 2002, the telecommunications industry remained mired in a deep slump. Nevertheless, Intervoice continued its mission to spread voice-enabled technology.

include all of Intervoice's offerings. In the future, Intervoice would offer Omvia prepaid/postpaid products; Omvia, which included messaging, unified messaging, and related products; the company's traditional enterprise business; and the portal products.

Within these categories, Intervoice would continue to offer the services it always had, including managed services for voice products. This market showed special promise in early 2003 as large corporations sought ways to benefit from speech technology but still hold costs down. To cater to this growing client base, which included *Fortune* 500 companies, Intervoice created a leasing option for its managed ASP services. Companies could lease equipment and management expertise instead of making large up-front capital investments.

Wireless communication, both in the United States and abroad, continued to be a strong potential source of revenue.

"Creating a leasing option for speech recognition technology is an important enabler for growth in the voice business market," noted *Datamonitor* analyst Benjamin Farmer. "Outsourcers must demonstrate value beyond the reduced up-front costs of the core technology. Intervoice's announcement of a contract with AdvancePCS and indications of a strong pipeline suggest its managed services offering is poised to take advantage of this market opportunity."[13]

Happy Twentieth

In 2003, Intervoice celebrated its twentieth anniversary. Hitting the twenty-year mark was no small accomplishment. Virtually every one of its competitors founded around the same time had either been bought or driven out of business. Intervoice was among the few to thrive in one of the world's most demanding, fast-changing industries. Along the way, the company had grown immensely and was fortunate to have strong leadership and a cadre of long-time, loyal employees.

In 2003, David Brandenburg led the Intervoice executive team to create a new mission and values statement, one that focused on growth, innovative communications solutions, and people.

The company's birthday was made even more rewarding by a flood of positive developments from Dallas. For example, the Michigan Department of Treasury reported that only four months after deploying Intervoice's system, 98 percent of incoming calls were handled by speech automation, droppings its cost per call from $1.65 to a mere 15 cents. Similarly, United Airlines reported savings of more than $25 million by using a speech-enabled flight information system. United's system dropped the cost per call from 65 cents to 16 cents.

These kinds of results were not uncommon, and they supported Intervoice's belief: Speech technology is easier, less expensive, and more efficient than any alternative. Furthermore, it is applicable in almost every industry. Travelocity, a Web travel retailer, experienced a 25 percent improvement in call volume with speech technology, while Manulife Financial, an insurance company, reported an 83 percent reduction in call duration and a 90 percent reduction in cost per call.

"We are hearing from our customers that speech-activated applications offer a compelling business case that is increasingly important to promoting profitability and customer satisfaction in these trying times," said Ritchey. "Speech solutions also provide new opportunities for revenue enhancement for our customers."[14]

In 2003, to bolster its research and development, Intervoice established a center at the University of Texas at Dallas to further the ease of use of voice technology and the humanization of automated conversation systems. The Intervoice Center for Automated Conversational Technologies has two permanent employees, a linguist, and a software engineer dedicated to its mission.

While enjoying its security and looking forward to growth once again, Intervoice used the early months of 2003 to craft a new mission statement. This statement declared that Intervoice would be "widely recognized for market and technology leadership by providing innovative communication software, services, and solutions to developers, enterprises, and carriers worldwide." This recognition would result from Intervoice's core values:

- Understand the needs of our employees, customers, and markets worldwide.
- Pursue continuous improvement in every aspect of our business practices.
- Provide the highest-quality products and services to our customers.
- Create distinct value for our employees, customers, and shareholders.
- Maintain leadership through innovation.
- Conduct business with honesty and integrity.

Together, the mission and core values united the company behind an ambitious vision that both recalled the past and presaged the future: "Intervoice technology leadership will shape the future by transforming the way people and information connect."[15]

"We're very excited," said Bob Ritchey. "The company is experiencing growth in its customer base and revenue, and the employment situation is stabilized. We've really turned the corner in a difficult market and are looking forward to strong growth in the future."[16]

NOTES TO SOURCES

Chapter One

1. Tim Jackson, *Inside Intel* (New York: Penguin Putnam Inc., 1996), p. 73.
2. "Inventors of the Modern Computer," About.com Web site, Inventors with Mary Bellis, http://inventors.about.com/library/weekly/aa033099.htm, July 2001.
3. Mike Tessarowicz, interview by Richard Hubbard, tape recording, 8 August 2001, Write Stuff Enterprises.
4. Dan Hammond, interview by Jeffrey Rodengen, tape recording, 8 May 2001, Write Stuff Enterprises.
5. Mike Tessarowicz, interview.
6. Skip Cave, interview by Richard Hubbard, tape recording, 5 May 2001, Write Stuff Enterprises.
7. Ibid.
8. Dan Hammond, interview.
9. Mike Tessarowicz, interview.
10. Tuan Nguyen, interview by Richard Hubbard, tape recording, 8 August 2001, Write Stuff Enterprises.
11. Cynthia Rivers, interview by Richard Hubbard, tape recording, 13 February 2001, Write Stuff Enterprises.
12. Don Crosbie, interview by Richard F. Hubbard, tape recording, 8 May 2001, Write Stuff Enterprises.
13. Ibid.
14. Ibid.
15. Chris Tessarowicz, interview by Richard Hubbard, tape recording, 8 August 2001, Write Stuff Enterprises.
16. Kathy Hackney, interview by Jeffrey L. Rodengen, tape recording, 9 May 2001, Write Stuff Enterprises.
17. Dwain Hammond, interview by Jeffrey L. Rodengen, tape recording, 8 May 2001, Write Stuff Enterprises.
18. Hackney, interview.
19. Ibid.
20. Al Fleener, interview by Jeffrey L. Rodengen, tape recording, 9 May 2001, Write Stuff Enterprises.
21. Ibid.
22. "ITA Debuts PBX Add-On Device," *PCExpo Today*, 24 September 1984.
23. Fleener, interview.
24. Ibid.
25. Marc Gardner, interview by Jeffrey L. Rodengen, tape recording, 8 May 2001, Write Stuff Enterprises.
26. Dan Hammond, interview.
27. Gardner, interview.
28. Fleener, interview.

29. Ibid.
30. Dan Hammond, interview.
31. Mike Tessarowicz, interview.
32. Hackney, interview.
33. Rivers, interview.
34. Nguyen, interview.
35. Dan Hammond, interview.

**Chapter One Sidebar:
Born to Tinker**

1. Dwain Hammond, interview.
2. Ibid.

**Chapter One Sidebar:
Tom Carter**

1. Mike Dano, "Thomas Carter: Creating Competition," *RCR Wireless News*, 7 May 2001.

Chapter Two

1. Gardner, interview.
2. Keith Gyssler, interview by Jeffrey L. Rodengen, tape recording, 7 May 2001, Write Stuff Enterprises.
3. Steve Coll, *The Deal of the Century: The Breakup of AT&T* (New York: Simon & Schuster Inc., 1986), p. 9.
4. "Betting on Chips," *Los Angeles Times*, 4 November 1990.
5. John Mascarenas, "Voice Messaging Creates New Dimension in Speech: The Ability to Talk without a Tongue," *Network World*, November 1984.
6. Pete Foster, interview by Richard Hubbard, tape recording, 8 August 2001, Write Stuff Enterprises.
7. Jim Bartimo, "InterVoice: Big Operators in Phone Answering Equipment," *Business Week*, 21 May 1990.
8. Brian Strachman, "IP Telephony Jumpstarts IVR," *Communications Solution Magazine*, January 2000.
9. Myra Hambleton, interview by Jeffrey L. Rodengen, tape recording, 18 May 2001, Write Stuff Enterprises.
10. Gordon Givens, interview by Richard Hubbard, tape recording, 9 May 2001, Write Stuff Enterprises.
11. Phil Walden, interview by Richard Hubbard, tape recording, 8 May 2001, Write Stuff Enterprises.
12. Ibid.
13. Dan Hammond, "Voice Automation Today," *Dallas-Fort Worth Technology*, November 1992, p. 3.
14. InterVoice Annual Report, 1989, p. 15.
15. InterVoice prospectus, 1989, p. 7.
16. Steven Vonder Harr, "InterVoice Heard on the Street: Investors Connect with 'Robot Operators,'" *Dallas Times Herald*, 11 October 1989.
17. Ibid.
18. InterVoice Annual Report, 1990, p. 15.

Chapter Three

1. David Brandenburg, interview by Jeffrey L. Rodengen, tape recording, 9 May 2001, Write Stuff Enterprises.
2. Ibid.
3. Ibid.
4. Ibid.
5. Mike Tessarowicz, interview.
6. David Both, "OS/2 History," *OS/2 Newsletter*, http/www.os2bbs.com/os2news/OS@History.html, August 2001.
7. Hambleton, interview.
8. Craig Evans, interview by Richard Hubbard, tape recording, 8 August 2001, Write Stuff Enterprises.
9. Dan Hammond, interview.
10. Gardner, interview.
11. Gyssler, interview.
12. "Warp Background," Harvard Computer Society, http//hcs.harvard.edu/~hcr/94oct/warpbg.html, August 2001.
13. InterVoice-Brite corporate website, http://www.InterVoice-brite.com/pressroom/exec_bios.html, August 2001.

14. Fleener, interview.
15. Dan Hammond interview, 8 May 2002.
16. Mike Barker, interview by Jeffrey L. Rodengen, tape recording, 7 May 2002, Write Stuff Enterprises.
17. Ibid.
18. Ibid.
19. Ibid.
20. Dean Howell, interview by Richard Hubbard, tape recording, 8 May 2001, Write Stuff Enterprises.
21. Walden, interview.
22. Ibid.
23. Joe Pietropaolo, interview by Richard Hubbard, tape recording, 8 August 2001, Write Stuff Enterprises.
24. Sean Silverthorne, "InterVoice's Dan Hammond: Moving Beyond Initial Success: and First Big Setback," *Investors' Business Daily*, 17 November 1992.
25. InterVoice Annual Report, 1992, p. 14.
26. John A. Jones, "InterVoice Finds New Ways to Call Computers by Phone," *Investor's Business Daily*, 26 October 1992.
27. "InterVoice," CEO Interviews, *Corporate Changes/Trends*, Wall Street Transcript Corporation, 19 October 1992, vol. 27, no. 3, p. CI-7276.
28. InterVoice Annual Report, 1993, p. 17.

29. Ibid., 16.
30. Barker, interview.
31. Ibid.
32. "InterVoice," CEO Interviews.
33. Ibid.
34. Ibid.
35. Kathleen Doler, "Computers & Automation," *Investor's Business Daily*, 17 September 1993.
36. Cave, interview.
37. Maurice Jones, "Small Resellers Eye Big Market," Telecommunications Online, http://www.telecoms-mag.com/issues/199711/tci/jones.html, August 2001.
38. Rob-Roy Graham, interview by Richard Hubbard, tape recording, 9 May 2001, Write Stuff Enterprises.
39. Givens, interview.
40. InterVoice Annual Report, 1994, p. 21.
41. Ibid.
42. Ibid.
43. InterVoice Annual Report, 1995, p. 3.
44. Frank Smith, "Friday the 13th Proves a Bad Day for InterVoice Stock Price," *Dallas Business Journal*, 23 July 1990.
45. Ibid.
46. Jennifer Files, "InterVoice Chairman Sells 600,000 Shares; Cuts Stake by 50%," *Dallas Morning News*, 28 September 1993.

47. Brandenburg interview, 9 May 2001.
48. InterVoice Annual Report, 1995, p. 18.
49. Bogdan Blaszczak, interview by Richard Hubbard, tape recording, 8 August 2001, Write Stuff Enterprises.
50. InterVoice Annual Report, 1994, p. 21.
51. Dwain Hammond, interview.
52. InterVoice Annual Report, 1995, p. 3.
53. Dan Hammond, interview.
54. Graham, interview.
55. Don Brown, interview by Richard Hubbard, tape recording, 9 May 2001, Write Stuff Enterprises.
56. Ibid.
57. Hackney, interview.
58. InterVoice Annual Report, 1994, p. 20.
59. "InterVoice," CEO Interviews.

Chapter Four

1. Larry Irving speech, "Voice on the Net: The Promise and Challenges Ahead," fall '98 Voice on the Net (Von) Conference, 17 September 1998.
2. InterVoice Annual Report, 1999, p. 10.
3. InterVoice Annual Report, 1997, p. 8.
4. Abhay Sawant, interview by Richard Hubbard, tape recording, 15 February

2002, Write Stuff Enterprises.

5. Maurice Jones, "Convergence Platforms," Telecommunications Online, http://www.telecoms-mag.com/issues/20000S/tci/converg/html, May 2000.

6. Bernard Levine, "Telecom Outsourcing Passion Grows," *Electronic News*, 26 February 2001.

7. Jones, "Convergence Platforms."

8. Irving, "Voice on the Net."

9. Gardner, interview.

10. InterVoice Annual Report, 1998, p. 3.

11. "InterVoice Establishes New Telecommunications Division," press release, 10 October 1994, InterVoice-Brite company archive.

12. Jersey Gilbert, Walecia Konrad, Robert Safian, James A. Anderson, Nellie S. Huang and Nelson Wang, "10 Stocks Under $20," *Smart Money*, March 1996, p. 87.

13. Ibid.

14. "Telecommunications Act of 1996," Localnet Communications Web site, www.gbso.net/luke/telact1.htm, August 2001.

15. Jason Cella, "Telecommunications Equipment,"

http://www.hoovers.com/industry/snapshot/profile/0,3519,57,00.html, August 2001.

16. Patrick Ross, "Remaking the Telecommunications Act," CNETNews.com Web site, http://news.cnet.com/news/0-1004-200-4718671.html, August 2001.

17. InterVoice Annual Report, 1998, p. 4.

18. Dan Hammond, interview.

19. Graham, interview.

20. Walden, interview.

21. Dan Hammond, interview.

22. Ibid.

23. Ibid.

24. InterVoice Annual Report, 1998, p. 2.

25. Ibid.

26. "InterVoice Adopts HP Opencall Platform for New Interactive Voice Services," press release, 7 May 1996, Intervoice company archive.

27. "InterVoice Purchases Call Center Product Suite From DC Systems," press release, 16 September 1998, Intervoice company archive.

28. Givens, interview.

29. Dan Hammond, interview.

30. InterVoice Annual Report, 1999, p. 1.

31. Givens, interview.

32. Paul Taylor, "The Power of Speech in the Digital Age: Voice Recognition," *Financial

Times Information Technology Review*, 2 June 1999.

33. Walt Mirkowicz, interview by Richard Hubbard, tape recording, 8 August 2001, Write Stuff Enterprises.

34. Taylor, "Power of Speech."

35. Ibid.

36. InterVoice Annual Report, 1998, p. 2.

37. Blaszczak, interview.

38. Cave, interview.

39. Ibid.

40. Hambleton, interview.

41. Maurice Jones, "Convergence Platforms."

42. "InterVoice Selected Again by Forbes Magazine as One of America's Best Small Companies," press release, 31 October 1995, Intervoice company archives.

43. InterVoice Annual Report, 1999, p. 1.

44. Ibid., p. 28.

Chapter Four Sidebar: Firsts

1. InterVoice Annual Report, 1998, p. 2.

Chapter Five

1. Lee Ann Groene, "The Ever-Restless Stan Brannan Chalks Up Big Success with Brite Voice," *Wichita Business Journal*, 9 October 1989, vol. 4, no. 31, sec. 1, p. 6.

2. Stan Brannan, interview by Richard Hubbard, tape recording, 9 August 2001, Write Stuff Enterprises.

3. Alex M. Cena, *The Voice Processing Industry* (William K. Woodruff & Company, 14 April 1990), p. 17.

4. Groene, "Ever-Restless Stan Brannan."

5. "Brite to Provide Initial 1,000 Port Gateway System," PR Newswire, 22 February 1989.

6. Ibid.

7. Groene, "Ever-Restless Stan Brannan."

8. Brannan interview, 9 August 2001.

9. Brite Voice Systems, Inc., 1989 Prospectus, Piper, Jaffray & Hopwood Inc. and B. C. Christopher Securities Co., 21 July 1989, p. 18.

10. Ibid.

11. Groene, "Ever-Restless Stan Brannan."

12. Brannan, interview.

13. Scott Walsh, interview by Richard Hubbard, tape recording, 9 August 2001, Write Stuff Enterprises.

14. Patrick Palmer, "Venture Capital Spurs Growth for Kansas Companies," *Wichita Business Journal*, 29 August 1988, vol. 3, no. 25, sec. 1, p. 13.

15. Lee Ann Groene, "Brite Voice Systems Breaks the Ice With $19 Million Public Offering," *Wichita Business Journal*, 18 September 1989, vol. 4, no. 28, sec. 1, p. 1.

16. Douglas S. Price, "Voice Information Sparks New Growth," Government Computer News, Cahners Publishing Associates, 1987.

17. Groene, "Brite Voice Systems Breaks the Ice."

18. Groene, "Ever-Restless Stan Brannan."

19. Ibid.

20. Groene, "Brite Voice Systems Breaks the Ice."

21. Glenn Etherington, interview by Richard Hubbard, tape recording, 20 February 2002, Write Stuff Enterprises.

22. Groene, "Brite Voice Systems Breaks the Ice."

23. Ibid.

24. Brannan, interview.

25. "Brite Voice Sells a Cityliner in San Francisco Area," PR Newswire, 17 November 1989.

26. Groene, "Brite Voice Systems Breaks the Ice."

27. Lee Ann Groene, "Brite Voice Systems Hopes to Raise $19.5 Million in Public Offering," *Wichita Business Journal*, 17 July 1989, vol. 4, no. 19, sec. 1, p. 1.

28. "Brite Voice Systems Installs a Telecare System at St. Paul Medical Center in Dallas," PR Newswire, 27 November 2001.

29. Lee Ann Groene, "Analysts Say Brite Voice Systems Stock Remains Strong Despite Drop-off," *Wichita Business Journal*, 6 November 1989, p. 7.

30. Ibid.

31. "Brite Voice Systems Sells 20 Systems to Marconi," PR Newswire, Wichita, Kansas dateline, 30 November 1989.

32. "Inc. Lists Fast-Growing Companies," *USA Today*, 17 April 1990, p. 5B.

33. Steven Shepard, *Telecommunications Convergence* (New York: McGraw-Hill, 2000), p. xvii.

34. "Brite Voice Grants Rights to Sell its Equipment in Sweden and Norway," PR Newswire, 7 August 1990.

35. Cena, *Voice Processing Industry*.

36. Groene, "Brite Voice Systems Hopes to Raise $19.5 Million."

37. "Brite Voice to Expand into Larger Facilities," PR Newswire, 2 March 1990.

38. Etherington, interview.

39. "To Our Stockholders," Brite Voice Systems Annual Report, 1991.

40. Ibid., p. 2.

41. Ibid.

42. Ibid.

43. "Brite Voice Reports Third Quarter Results," PR Newswire, 23 October 1991.

Chapter Six

1. "To Our Stockholders,"Brite Voice Systems Annual Report, 1992.
2. Erwin Selba, "Brite Voice Systems Rethinking its Way of Doing Business," *Wichita Business Journal*, 3 September 1993, p. 4.
3. Brite Voice Systems Annual Report, 1992, p. 4.
4. Ibid.
5. Etherington, interview.
6. Brite Voice Systems Annual Report, 1993, p. 1.
7. Ibid.
8. Brite Voice Systems Annual Report, 1994, p. 1.
9. Ted Sickinger, "'94 Tough on Regional Stocks," *Kansas City Star*, 7 January 1995, p. B1.
10. "To Our Stockholders," Brite Voice Systems Annual Report, 1994.
11. Ibid.
12. Ibid., p. 5.
13. Ibid., p. 3.
14. "To Our Stockholders," Brite Voice Systems Annual Report, 1995.
15. Ibid.
16. Ibid.
17. Ibid.
18. Ibid.
19. Victor Wisna, "Entrepreneurs of the Year for Region are Announced," *Kansas City Business Journal*, 30 June 1995.
20. "Captain of His Fate," *Wichita Commerce*, November 1990, p. 12.
21. David Dinell, "Brite Voice Grows with Technology and Buyouts," *Wichita Business Journal*, 15 March 1996, p. 8B.
22. Jennifer Mann Fuller, "Battered Brite Voice is Undervalued, Analyst Says," *Kansas City Star*, 11 August 1996, p. F7.
23. Dinell, "Brite Voice Grows with Technology and Buyouts."
24. Jennifer Mann Fuller, "Bullish on Telecommunications; Industry Deregulation Paves the Way for Big Returns, Analyst Says," *Kansas City Star*, 23 February 1996, p. D23.
25. "Brite's Voice Messaging Services Cross the Atlantic, Ready to Compete in North American Wireless Markets," PR Newswire, 25 March 1996.
26. "Ameritech and BellSouth Deploy Voice Control Systems' Cellular Speech Recognition Technology," Business Wire, 18 April 1996.
27. "Contract for $7 Million Signed This Week; Cellnet Order is Largest in Brite Voice Systems' History," PR Newswire, 21 August 1996.
28. Form 10-K, Brite Voice Systems, 1996, p. 11.
29. Brite Voice Systems Annual Report, 1997.
30. Form 10-K, Brite Voice, 1996, p. 12.
31. "Brite's Year-End 1996 Record Revenues of $110.4 million; New Service Products Under Way," PR Newswire, 10 February 1997.
32. Karissa Boney, "Pumping Resources Into Prepaid," *Wireless World*, September 1997.
33. Brite Voice Systems Annual Report, 1997, p. 4.
34. "Brite Voice Systems Partners with Sprint PCS for New Service," PR Newswire, 10 September 1997.
35. Brite Voice Systems Annual Report, 1997, p. 4.
36. Blake Fontenay, "Brite Voice Plans to Fill 200 More," *Orlando Sentinel*, 17 January 1998, p. B-1.
37. Roz Hutchinson, "Easy Access, Lower Taxes Key to Brite Execs' Move to Florida," *Wichita Business Journal*, 6 June 1997, p. 1.
38. Brannan, interview.
39. Hutchinson, "Easy Access, Lower Taxes Key."
40. "Brite 2nd Quarter Net Loss of $4.9 Million," PR Newswire, 22 July 1997.
41. Form 10-K, Brite Voice Systems, 1997, p. 2.

42. Blake Fontenay, "Brite Voice Plans to Fill 200 More."

43. Scott Walsh, interview by Richard Hubbard, tape recording, 8 May 2001, Write Stuff Enterprises.

44. Form 10-K, Brite Voice Systems, 1997, p. 20.

45. Brite Voice Systems Annual Report, 1997.

46. "Shareholder Letter," Brite Voice Systems Annual Report, 1998.

47. "Brite Names David S. Gergacz Chairman of the Board," PR Newswire, 12 January 1998.

48. "Brite Voice," *Investor's Business Daily*, 2 June 1998.

49. Dianne Hammer, "Asia-Pacific Carriers Working to Retain Customer Base," *Global Wireless*, March-April 1998, p. 2.

50. "Brite Voice in $15M Pact To Provide Voice-Activated Dialing," Dow Jones News Service, Dow Jones News, 28 September 1998.

51. Jerry Jackson, "Brite Voice's Chief Resigns; Management Styles Appear to Be Reason for Departure," *Orlando Sentinel*, 17 November 1998, p. C1.

52. Brannan, interview.

53. Walsh, interview, 8 May 2001.

54. "Brite Voice to Sell Unit for $15 Million," *Reuter Financial Report*, 18 September 1998.

55. Ray Naeini, interview by Richard Hubbard, tape recording, 8 May 2001, Write Stuff Enterprises.

56. "Shareholder Letter," Brite Voice Systems Annual Report, 1998.

57. Walsh, interview, 8 May 2001.

58. "Voice Control Systems Signs Multi-Year Contract with Brite Voice Systems for Next-Generation Speech Recognition Technology," PR Newswire, 25 January 1999.

59. "Brite's Prepaid Solutions Now Used by Over Two Million Subscribers; Prepaid Managed Service Exceeds One Million Subscriber Milestone," Business Wire, 15 April 1999.

60. Naeini, interview, 8 May 2001.

Chapter Six Sidebar: Recruiting

1. Blake Fontenay, "Brite Voice Puts New Twist on Recruiting," *Orlando Sentinel*, 23 April 1998.

2. Ibid.

Chapter Seven

1. Etherington, interview.

2. Brannan, interview.

3. Graham, interview.

4. "InterVoice and Brite to Merge," press release, 27 April 1999, Intervoice company archive.

5. Ibid.

6. "InterVoice Completes Merger with Brite Voice Systems," press release, 13 August 1999, Intervoice company archive.

7. "InterVoice Officially Changes Name to InterVoice-Brite, Inc.," press release, 18 August 1999, Intervoice company archive.

8. "InterVoice Completes Merger."

9. Ibid.

10. Dennis Pearce, "Dallas Company Buys Brite Voice Inc.," *Wichita Eagle*, 28 April 1999.

11. Brown, interview.

12. Ibid.

13. Hackney, interview.

14. Greg Groeller, "Brite Voice Bought by Competitor," *Orlando Sentinel*, 28 April 1999.

15. USBancorp Piper Jaffray Equity Research Notes, InterVoice Inc., 28 April 1999.

16. Jonathan Weil, "InterVoice Sell-Off May Have Been Overdone in Light of Its Prospects," *Wall Street Journal*, 19 May 1999.

17. USBancorp Piper Jaffray Equity Research Notes.

18. Groeller, "Brite Voice Bought by Competitor."
19. Donald Newman and Joshua Hantman, "INTV-InterVoice & Brite Announce Merger Agreement," Ladenburg Thalman Morning Meeting Note, 28 April 1999.
20. Graham, interview.
21. Naeini, interview.
22. Dwain Hammond, interview.
23. Givens, interview.
24. InterVoice-Brite Annual Report, 2000, p. 2.
25. Mirkowicz, interview.
26. Newman and Hantman, "INTV-InterVoice & Brite Announce Merger Agreement."
27. Graham, interview.
28. "InterVoice-Brite Identified as World Leader in IVR," press release, 21 September 1999, InterVoice-Brite company archive.
29. Ibid.
30. InterVoice-Brite Annual Report, 2000, p. 1.
31. Victor Godinez, "InterVoice Stock Falls on Notice; Earnings Unlikely to Reach Projections, Dallas Firm Warns," Dallas Morning News, 8 June 2000.
32. Brandenburg, interview, 9 May 2001.
33. "Hammond to Resign as InterVoice-Brite Chairman," press release, 16 October 2001, InterVoice-Brite company archive.
34. Brandenburg, interview, 9 May 2001.
35. Givens, interview.
36. Hambleton, interview.
37. "InterVoice-Brite Announces Organization Changes," press release, 6 December 2000, InterVoice-Brite company archive.
38. Brandenburg, interview, 9 May 2001.
39. InterVoice-Brite Annual Report, 2000, p. 1.

Chapter Eight

1. David Christofides, "Telecom by the Numbers," Dismal Scientist Web site, http://www.dismal.com/thoughts/telecomm.stm, September 2001.
2. Ibid.
3. John Borland, "Telecom Players Spend Big, but Win Little," News.com Website, http://news.cnet.com/news/0-1004-200-2878444.html?tag=rltdnws, September 2001.
4. Patrick Ross, Corey Grice, and John Borland, "2000 Market Tumultuous Times for Telecom Companies," News.com Website, http://news.cnet.com/news/0-1004-200-4228141.html?tag=bplst, September 2001.
5. Ibid.
6. Ibid.
7. Ibid.
8. "InterVoice-Brite's OneVoice Platform Wins Product of the Year Award from C@ll Center CRM Solutions Magazine," press release, 18 January 2000, InterVoice-Brite company archive.
9. "InterVoice to Showcase Speech Recognition Technology at CALLcenterDEMO99," press release, 3 February 1999, InterVoice-Brite company archive.
10. "InterVoice Unveils Breakthrough Development Software for Speech Recognition," press release, 12 August 1999, InterVoice-Brite company archive.
11. "InterVoice and SpeechWorks Announce the Availability of SpeechAccess Phonetic Speech Recognition Products for Windows NT," press release, 24 June 1999, InterVoice-Brite company archive.
12. "SpeechWorks Users Trade In Their Technology," *Wall Street &*

Technology, Miller Freeman Inc., 1 March 1999.
13. Curt Harler, "Speech Recognition Tools Get Standards, Respect," *Business Communications Review*, 1 May 2000.
14. Mirkowicz, interview.
15. "InterVoice-Brite Adds New Capabilities to Advanced Speech Recognition Product," press release, 9 May 2000, InterVoice-Brite company archive.
16. "Consumers Embrace Speech Recognition; Study Results Indicate Increasing Mass Appeal and Consumer Acceptance of Voice Web and V-Commerce Applications," PR Newswire, 9 October 2000.
17. "InterVoice-Brite Broadens Speech Capabilities of SpeechAccess Product Line," press release, 17 July 2001, InterVoice-Brite company archive.
18. "InterVoice-Brite Announces Enhanced XML Support," press release, 5 September 2000, InterVoice-Brite company archive.
19. Evans, interview.
20. Brian Strachman, "Voice-XML—A Crisis for IVR," *Communications Solutions*, October 2000.

21. "Adoption of VoiceXML Standard," *Electronic Commerce News*, 12 June 2000.
22. Cave, interview.
23. "InterVoice-Brite Enhances OneVoice Product."
24. Sawant, interview.
25. "InterVoice-Brite Grosses $21.4 Million on Sale of SpeechWorks Stock," press release, 13 February 2001, InterVoice-Brite company archive.
26. "Market Guide: Significant Developments Report for InterVoice-Brite, Inc.," Multex.com Web site, http://yahoo.market-guide.c.../signdevt.asp?ns s=yahoo&rt=signdevt&rn= 4/10, September 2001.
27. Naeini, interview.
28. "Omvia Technology Will End the Digital Divide," press release, 13 February 2001, InterVoice-Brite company archive.
29. InterVoice-Brite Annual Report, 2001.
30. "Market Guide: Significant Developments Report."
31. "InterVoice-Brite Announces VoiceXML Capabilities."
32. Walsh, interview, 8 May 2001.
33. Maurice Jones, "Convergence Platforms."

34. InterVoice-Brite Annual Report, 2001.
35. Ibid.
36. "InterVoice-Brite and 724 Solutions Team Up to Bring Voice to the Wireless Internet," press release, 24 September 2001, InterVoice-Brite company archive.
37. "David Brandenburg," *CEO/CFO Interviews*, interview by Walter Banks, January 2001.
38. David Brandenburg, interview by Jeffrey L. Rodengen and Richard Hubbard, tape recording, 10 January 2002, Write Stuff Enterprises.
39. Paula Felps, "Dollars for Dialing," *Dallas Morning News*, 12 March 2001.
40. "Letter from CEO," InterVoice-Brite Annual Report, 2001.
41. Ibid.
42. Ibid., p. 9.
43. Ibid., p. 10.
44. Ibid.
45. Christine Holley, "Unified Communications: A New Solution for a New Millennium," excerpt from INTUG—the International Telecommunications Users Group, Update 1999/2000, Kensington Publications Limited.
46. "InterVoice-Brite Strengthens Asia-Pacific Presence with Opening of Japan Office," press

release, 12 March 2001, InterVoice-Brite company archive.

47. Ibid.

48. Ibid.

49. Form 10-K, InterVoice-Brite Annual Report, 2001, p. 10.

50. Ibid.

51. Ibid.

52. "David Brandenburg," *CEO/CFO Interviews*.

53. "InterVoice-Brite Provides Speech-Based Bank-by-Phone Application for Major Worldwide Financial Institution," press release, 16 January 2001, InterVoice-Brite company archive.

54. "InterVoice-Brite Technology Is the Power behind Turkey's First Speech Recognition System," press release, 23 July 2001, InterVoice-Brite company archive.

55. "Omvia Achieves Ericsson Certification," press release, 2 October 2001, InterVoice-Brite company archive.

56. "David Brandenburg," *CEO/CFO Interviews*.

57. Naeini, interview.

58. "BT/Cellnet Extends Contract with InterVoice-Brite," press release, 7 June 2001, InterVoice-Brite company archive.

59. Ibid.

60. "InterVoice-Brite Expands Its End-to-End Solutions with the Launch of Omvia Professional Services," press release, 8 October 2001, InterVoice-Brite company archive.

61. Christine Holley, "Unified Communications: A New Solution."

62. Graham, interview.

63. Holley, "Unified Communications: A New Solution."

64. Ibid.

65. Andrew Fisher, "New Ways to Win Over Fickle Clients," *Financial Times Limited*, 17 October 2001.

66. George Platt Sr., interview by Richard Hubbard, tape recording, 8 August 2001, Write Stuff Enterprises.

Chapter Nine

1. David Brandenburg, interview by Richard Hubbard and Jon VanZile, tape recording, 27 June 2002, Write Stuff Enterprises.

2. Ibid.

3. Ibid.

4. "Microsoft/InterVoice Strategic Alliance Q&A," InterVoice internal documents, Intervoice corporate archive.

5. Barbara Marlet, "The Impact of Our Strategic Alliance with Microsoft," Intervoice corporate archive.

6. Press release, Intervoice corporate archive, summer 2002.

7. "Microsoft/InterVoice Startegic Alliance Q&A."

8. Ibid.

9. Mike Polcyn, interview by Jon VanZile, tape recording, 28 June 2002, Write Stuff Enterprises.

10. Bob Ritchie, interview by Richard Hubbard and Jon VanZile, tape recording, 3 July 2002, Write Stuff Enterprises.

11. Ritchey, employee newsletter, "2002 in Review," Intervoice corporate archive.

12. Ritchey, interview by Jon VanZile, tape recording, 7 January 2003, Write Stuff Enterprises.

13. Benjamin Farmer, "Industry Analysts' Perspectives," Intervoice corporate archive.

14. Ritchey, "2002 in Review."

15. Intervoice Mission, Values, and Vision statements, Intervoice corporate archive, 2003.

16. Ritchey, "2002 in Review."

INDEX

Page numbers in italics indicate photographs.

1-800-COLLECT, 63, 64, 66
900 Services, 83, 86, 87

A

acquisitions and mergers
    Brite Voice, 88, 92–95
    Brite Voice and InterVoice, 75,
        102–103, 105, *106*
    InterVoice, 53, 56, 69
Adelphia, 129
AdvancePCS, 135, 136
Aetna, 38
Agent Connect, 48, 69, 118
AlliedSignal, 79
ALTech, 73
America First Credit Union, 135
American Banking Association
    trade show, *31*
American Express, 38
Ameritech, 99
analog interface/3, *49*
Apollo project, 62, 66–67, *67*
Armstrong, C. Michael, 101, 117
artificial intelligence, 73–74
ASPs (application service
    providers), 62, 112,
    124–125
ASR (automatic speech
    recognition), 49–50
Associated Press Stockquote Wire,
    82
AT&T
    1982 breakup, 29–30
    and Carterfone, 25

as customer, 100, 109
    recruiting AT&T employees,
        101
    Telecommunications Act of
        1996, 63–64
    and telecommunications
        industry, 38, 49, 61, 62,
        117–118
AT&T Wireless, 99
Avaya, 123
awards and recognition
    Brite Voice, 87, 88–89, 93, 96,
        100
    InterVoice, 58, 74
    InterVoice-Brite, 112, 114, 118

B

Bank of America, 108
banking industry, 20–23, 29,
    31–34, 124
Barker, Mike, 45–46, 48, 56, *57*,
    66, *67*
Bartlett, Steve, *55*
B.C. Christopher Securities, 83, 86
Bean, Alan, 67, *67*
Bell Canada, 89
BellSouth, 99
Berger, David, 66, *71*, 74, 109,
    113, 115
Blackwelder, Barry, *35*
Blair, D. H., 23
Blaszczak, Bogdan, 34, 53, 73
board of directors, 24, 38, 44–45,
    108

Boe, Barbie, *37*
Bonet, Louis, 50
Booth, David, 76, *113*
Boyle, David, *35*
Brandenburg, David, *43, 55, 114,*
    130, 134, 137
    as CEO, InterVoice-Brite,
        114–115, 118, 127–128
    contract extension, 53
    early years at InterVoice,
        41–45
    and restructuring, 131–132
    retirement, 66
    as vice chairman of InterVoice,
        56, 58
    and VoicePlex acquisition, 56
    on wireless technology, 122
Brandenburg, Diana, 41, *134*
Brannan, Scott, *81*
Brannan, Stan, *76, 78, 80, 98,*
    104
    founding of Brite Voice, 79–82
    and InterVoice-Brite merger,
        101–103, *107*,
        107–109
    leadership, 96
    and Perception Technology
        Corp. merger, 92
Brannan, Sue, *102*
Brite Digital Systems, 79
Brite Voice, founding of, 79–82
BriteConnect, 100
BriteDebit, 100
BriteESP, 100
BriteTalk, 100

British Telecom, 62, 63
Brown, Charlie, 30
Brown, Don, 58, 75, 109
BT/Cellnet, *113*, 125
Burnet, John, *76*
Business Week, 42
Butler, Gerald, 97
BVSG (Brite Voice Systems Group Ltd.), 88, 91

C

Cahners, 74
Cahners In-Stat Group, 112
California First Bank, *33*
Call Center, 74
CallingCard, 20
CANTV, 53
CANTX, 63
Carter, Helen, *55*
Carter, Tom, 24, 25, *25*, 38, *39*
Carter Building, *54–55*, 56
Carterfone, 13, 25
CASP group, 121, 124
Cave, Skip, 15, 46, 49–50, 73, *120*, 120
Cellular One, 99
Centrelink, 135
Chase Manhattan Bank, 69
Christal, David, *50*
Chronicle Publishing Co., 83
CIN, 82
CITYLINE, 80, 82, 83
Clayton, John, *35*
C@ll Center CRM Solutions, 112, 118
Clydesdale Bank, 36
Commercial Federal Corp, 82
Communications Solutions EXPO, 118
Comverse Technology, 123
Condray, Mickey, *35*
CPE, 53
CRM market, 125
Crosbie, Don, *18*, *31*, *37*, *39*, *43*, *55*
    retirement, 46
    as sales and marketing director, 17–18, 21, 24
CTI, 69
CTI Magazine, 100

D

Data Resource System, *30*
DataConnect, 36
Datamonitor, 62

Dataquest, 74
Davox, 49, 69
DCT Standards Committee, 59
DDI, 99
Derrick Edge, *77*
Deutsche Telekom, 62
Dialogic, 17, 38
Digital Systems, 49
distribution, 49
divestitures, 102, 121
Donaldson, John, 133, *135*
DowPhone, 82
Dragon Systems, 71
DSC Communicatins, 63
DSP (digital signal processor), 35
Durbeck, Martin, 17, 19, *19*
Durlacher Research, 62
Dvox, 15

E

EDS, 20, 29, 38
electronic publishing business, 99
EMEA operation, 101
Empire Savings, 24
employee events
    Brite Voice, 97
    InterVoice, *45*, 66, *66*, *70*, *71*, *75*
Enron, 129
Enterprise Solutions Division, 115, 124, 128, *128*, 131
Entre Computer Centers, 41
Ericsson, 109, 124
ESP (Enhanced Services Platform), 69
Etherington, Glenn, *83*, *90*, *99*
    and acquisitions, 88, 92
    and BriteVoice IPO, 83
    as CFO, 97
    and InterVoice merger, 107
    relocation to Orlando, 99
E*Trade, 73, 109
Evans, Craig, *35*, 41–42, 43, 120, *120*
Excel, 129
Exxon, 19

F

Farmer, Benjamin, 136
Farris, Victoria, 97
fax products, 89
FBU concept, 91
Ferber, Leon, *90*, 92, *92*
Ferranti Business Communications, 88

First Alabama Bank, *32*
First Albany, 96
First Analysis, 96
First Interstate Bancorp, 38
First Union, 63
Fisher, Andrew, 125
Fleener, Al, *31*, *34*, *39*, *43*
    and David Brandenburg, 41
    and IPO, 23–24
    joins InterVoice, 19–20, 21
    marketing to banks, 29, 32
    named president, 34
    retirement, 44
Fleener, Marjorie, *35*
Fone Tower, 37, *38*
Forbes, 58, 74
Ford Credit, 109
Foster, Pete, 31
France, Robert, *64*
Friedberg, Tom, 86
Frost & Sullivan, 74, 96, 112, 114

G

Gardner, Marc, 21, 22–23, *26*, *34*, 44, 62, 63
Gateway 5000, 80, 83, 87
General Electric, 36
GeoTel Communications, 69
Gergacz, David, *97*, 97–98, 100–101, 107
Givens, Gordon, *18*
    career at InterVoice, 34, 75
    international business, 51
    and IVR technology, 70
    and merger, 112, 115
    on product quality, 41
    and Y2K, 69
Global Crossing, 129
Gold, Terry, 120
Gold Systems, 120
Gorka, Gene, *35*
Graham, Rob-Roy, *57*, *110*
    and All-Star Band, 66
    and banking customers, 125
    on executive team, 74–75
    joins InterVoice, 46
    and merger, 108, 109, 111, 112
    and Paris office, 50–51
    and restructuring, 131
Granville, Joe, 101
Greene, Harold H., 89
GTE, 53, 63, 94
GTECH, 14, 24, 26
Gtrzinek, Gary, *31*
Gyssler, Keith, 18, 29, 38, 44, *58*

H

Hackney, Kathy, *34, 58*
    early years at InterVoice, 18, 19, 21
    and merger, 110
    named benefits manager, 58
    on new headquarters, 24
Hallam, Stuart, 97
Hambleton, Myra, *108*
    on artificial intelligence, 73–74
    early years at InterVoice, 33–34
    and merger, 115
    on OS/2 conversion, 42–43
Hamilton, Elliott, 117
Hammond, Carol, *16, 61*
Hammond, Dan, *14, 18, 19, 34, 37, 39, 41, 43, 47, 50, 51, 55, 57, 65, 70, 75, 105, 111, 113*
    early career, 13–15
    family, *16, 22, 22, 61*
    founding of InterVoice, 17–23
    and IPO, 23–26
    as manager, 47
    and merger, *107*
    named CEO, 34
    named chairman, 44–45
    and OS/2 conversion, 42–44
    retires as CEO, 114
    and Tom Carter, 24
    and Viper and Apollo projects, 67, *67*
    on voice response applications, 36
Hammond, Dwain, *61, 64*
    on executive team, 75, *75*
    family, *16, 22, 22*
    joins InterVoice, 18, 21
    on MCI order, 53
    and merger, 112
    and One Voice, 48
Hammond, Holly, *18, 75*
Hammond, Mac, *22, 22, 61*, 127
Hammond, Volina, *16*, 22, *61*
Hammond, William, *16*, 22, *61*
Hammond Computer Products, 14
HCA Wesley Hospital, 81
headquarters buildings
    Brite Voice, *81, 84–86*, 88, 99, *100*
    InterVoice, 24, *26, 36, 37*, 38, *54–55*, 56
    InterVoice-Brite, *116, 123*

Hemmings, David, *90*, 97
Henrich, Mike, *95*
Herrman, Dick, 70
Hewlett-Packard, 61, 69
Howell, Dan, 46
Howell, Dean, 75
Howell, Wendell, 20–21
Huber, Lee, *64*
Hunter, Chier, *99*

I

IBM, 23–24, 35, 42, 44, 71
In-Stat Group, 74
Inc. magazine, 87
Infovox AB, 87
Integrated Telephony Products, 69
Intel, 94
InterAction, *108*
Interactive Technology Associates (later InterVoice), 17–23
InterGen, 35
International Business, 88–89
international markets
    Brite Voice, 80, 82, 87, 91–93, 95, 99, 101
    InterVoice, 36, 50–53, 63, 70, 74
    InterVoice-Brite, 112, 123
Internet Resources, 94
InterSoft, 67
InterTalk, 23
InterVoice, founding of, 17–23
Intervoice Center for Automated Conversational Technologies, 137
InterVoice (programming language), 17
InterVoice S.A., 50–51
InVision, 112, *118*
ISDN-PRI, 37
ISO 9001, 62–63, *63*
IT Network, 99
ITI, 20
Ivester, Rodney, *35*
IVR technology, 13, 15, 70–71, 73, 89, 118–119, *120*

J, K, L

J. C. Penney, 38
James, Victor, 75
Jansen, Erik, 53
Jones, Mark, 63

Kansas City Star, 93
Klumpp, Brian, 101

Knapp, Carol Hammond, *16*, 22, *22*
Knight-Ridder, 83
Koening, Peter, 35, *35*
Kozarsky, Karl, 38
KWCH-TV, 83

LDDS, 53, 63
leasing option, 136
Lernout & Hauspie, 71
Line of Business structure, 132
logos
    Brite Voice, *79*
    InterVoice, *13*
    Omvia, 121
    RobotOperator, 29
London Financial Times, 94
Lucent, 134

Maitland, Dan, 92
Maltz, Alan, 97
managed services, 89, 91, 92, 93, 103
management team, *48*
manufacturing operations, 35, 46, *126*
Manulife Financial, 137
Marconi Company Ltd., 36, 82, 86
marketing strategy, 19–20, 23–24
Martin, David, 81
MasterCard International, 69
MCI, 38, 53, 63, 64, 66, 94
MediaConnect, 63
Mehler, Dean, 79
Melita, 49
Mergenthaler Linotype, 79
merger of Brite Voice and InterVoice, 75, 102–103, 105, *106*
    cultural differences of companies, 109–110
    market leadership, 112
    name change to Intervoice, 132
    reaction to, 109, 110–111
Metrocel Cellular Telephone Co., 92
Michigan Department of Treasury, 135, 137
Michigan Lottery, 14
MicroChannel, 48
Microsoft, 133
Miniphone, 99
Mirkowicz, Walt, 34–35, *35*, 42, 71, 112, 119
mission statement, 137

Mitchell, Beverly, *35*
Mondex Gateway, 69
Morrison, John, 79, 81
Mounday, Don, 88
MS-DOS, 42–44
Mycro-Tek, 79

N

Naeini, Ray, *102, 113*
    on ASP model, 124–125
    on growth of BriteVoice, 102,
       103
    and merger, 109, 110, 112
    and Network Solutions
       Division, 115
    on Omvia, 121
    relocation to Orlando, 99
Naeini, Shahin, *102*
name changes, 23, 132
NATA (North American
      Telecommunications
      Assn.), 25
National Data Corp., 38
National Westminsters Bank, 38
NationsBank, *32*
Natural Microsystems, 17
NEC, 69
Neiman Marcus, 135
Network Solutions Division, 115,
      123–125, 127, 131
New York Times, 94
NewNet, 69
Newsline, *88*
Nguyen, Tuan, 17, 18, 21, *21, 26,*
      27, 35
Nortel Networks, 123
Northern Telecom, 49
NSP 5000 systems, 70, *124*
Nuance Communications, 73,
      118–119

O, P, Q

Octel, 49
Omvia, 121–122, 125, 135–136
OneVoice, 37, 48, 53, 58, 69, 118
operating systems, 35, 42–44, 62
OS/2 conversion, 42–44
Owens, Ron, 119
Oxman, Jason, 25

Pantagraph, 83
patents, 46
Patterson, Stuart, 119
PCExpo Show, 19

Perception Technology Corp., 38,
      92–93
Periphonics, 19, 38, 61
Philips, 71
Pietropaolo, Joseph, 38, 44, 47
Piper, Jaffray & Hopwood, 86, 110
Platt, George Sr., 44, 45, 125
Polcyn, Mike, 18, 35, *35*, 46, 75,
      134
Polsky, Steve, 63
Pratt, Eric, 75
predictive dialer, 15
prepaid wireless market, 98–99,
      103
Preston State Bank, 20–22
Probe Research, 38, 87

QVC, 94, 94–95
Qwest, 129

R

Radiofone, 99
RBOCs, 30, 53, 63, 89, 94
Real Estate Hotline, 81
RealCareRemote, 69
recession of 2001, 115, 117–118
restructuring, 115, 127–128,
      131–132
Rhetorics, 17
Ritchey, Bob, *128, 131*
    and bank customers, 124
    hired by InterVoice-Brite, 115
    as president of InterVoice-
      Brite, 132, 134–135, 137
    restructuring, 128
Rivers, Ed, 17, 21, 24, *26*
Robertson, Stephens & Co., 53
RobotOperator, 20, 22, *29, 31–33,*
      32–37
Rockwell, 36, 44
Rogers Cantel, 99
Rolm, 49
Runyan, Larry, 79
Rutherford, Jeff, *58*

S

Safaricom, 135
SALT (Speech Application
      Language Tags), 133–134
Sattar, Sohail, 63
Sawant, Abhay, 121
Schmuking, Werner, *50, 51*
Scott, Mark, 91, 96
September 11, 2001, tragedy, 127

7-Eleven, 15–17, 19
Shapiro, Florence, *55*
Siemens, *50*, 63, 70
Siemens Private Communications
      Systems Group, 53
Smith, Harold, 96
Smith, Ron, 83
Social Security Administration, 36,
      38
Southland, 15–17, 19
speech recognition technology, 70,
      118–119. *see also* IVR
      technology
SpeechAccess, 73, 118–119
Speechify TTS, 119
Speechworks, 71, 73, 118–119,
      121
Splitt, Becky, 89
Sprint, 38, 63, 83, 94, 117–118
Sprint Gateways, 87
Sprint PCS, 99, 109, 112
St. Paul Medical Center, 86
Stephenson, Scott, 86
stock (Brite Voice)
    initial public offering, 82–83
    and merger, 108
    performance, 93, 96, 101
stock (InterVoice)
    initial public offering, 23–24,
      26
    and merger, 108
    performance, 36–37, 38, 53
secondary offering, 1989, 38
splits, 53
stock (InterVoice-Brite), 114, 129
Stockford, Paul, 112
StockQuote Hotline, 80
Strachman, Brian, 120, 133–134
Strategis Group, 117
Strzinek, Gary, *58*
Sungard, 69
SunTrust, 135
Syntech, 13–15
Syntellect, 38

T

talking yellow pages, 81
Tannenbaum, David, 46
TBS (Telephone Broadcast
      Systems), 15
TDP, 99
Telecare, 81, 86
Telecom Business, 114
Telecom Equipment Pte Ltd., 53
Telecommunication of Denver, 80

Telecommunications Act of 1996, 63–64, 96
telecommunications industry, 11, 61–64, 117
TELE*MASTER, 73
Telfonica, 95
Telia, 99
Tessarowicz, Chris, 17, 18, *19*
Tessarowicz, Mike, 13–15, *19, 21,* 34, *39,* 44
Texas Instruments, 31
Time Communications, 89
Times Mirror, 83
Tinger, Herbert, 96
Touch-Talk, 94–95
trade shows, *60*
Transaction Technologies, 14
Travelocity, 137
Tribune Newspapers, 94
Trippi, Frank, *92*
TSL, 94–95

U, V

United Airlines, 137
U.S. Order, 69

U.S. West, 53, 63

VCS distributor conference, *108*
VCS (voice control systems), 31, 36
Viper project, 62, 66–67
VisualConnect, 63
VMX, 49
VocalCard, *12,* 37, *47*
Voice Control Systems, 96–97, 103
Voice Directory, 83
Voice Information Associates, 49–50, 73
VoiceChannel architecture, 48
VoiceDial, 31, 36
VoicePlex Corp, 53, 56
VoiceQuote, 36
VoiceSelect, *91,* 93, 95, 97
VoiceTone Dialer, 92
Votan, 31
Votrax, 38
VSD (Voice Systems Director), 91, 93, 95
VSG (Voice Systems Group), 88
VXML, 119–121, 134

W, Y

Walden, Phil, *14,* 35, *35,* 46, 75
Walsh, Marie, *93*
Walsh, Scotty, *76, 90, 93*
  and acquisitions, 88, 92
  early years at BriteVoice, 82
  on executive team, 98, 100
  and merger, 102, 109, 110
  on Omvia, 122
  relocation to Orlando, 99
Weeren, Eric, 48
Westcott, Rick, 21, 26
WilTel, 69
Windows operating system, 42–44
wireless market, 99–100, 122
Wireless One, 99
Woodruff, William, 38, 44
Worcester Telegram and Gazette, 83
WorldCom, 117–118, 129

XML, 119–121

Yankee Group, 98
Y2K, 69, 114